THE JUMBO BOOK OF NATURE SCIENCE

Kids Can Press Ltd. acknowledges with appreciation the
assistance of the Canada Council and the Ontario Arts Council
in the production of this book.

Canadian Cataloguing in Publication Data

Hickman, Pamela
   The jumbo book of nature science

Includes index.
ISBN 1-55074-317-1

1. Nature study — Juvenile literature.
2. Scientific recreations — Juvenile literature.
I. Shore, Judie.   II. Federation of Ontario Naturalists.   III. Title.

QH48.H53 1996   j508   C96-930736-8

FEDERATION OF
Ontario Naturalists

Kids Can Press Ltd.
29 Birch Ave.
Toronto, Ontario, Canada
M4V 1E2

The material in this book originally
appeared in *Birdwise*, *Bugwise* and
Plantwise.

Printed and bound in Canada
Text stock contains over 50%
recycled paper   96 0 9 8 7 6 5 4 3 2 1

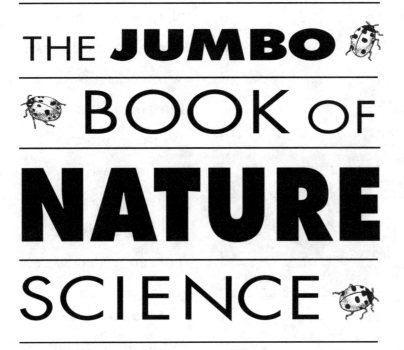

THE JUMBO BOOK OF NATURE SCIENCE

written by Pamela Hickman and
the Federation of Ontario Naturalists
illustrated by Judie Shore

Kids Can Press Ltd.
Toronto

Contents

Outdoor Adventures

Take a walk on the wild side and discover some of the incredible creatures that live at your doorstep and down the street. Whether you live in the city or country, you'll find bugs, plants and birds to watch, sketch and photograph. Learn some tricks for attracting bugs, find out what's living in and on tree leaves, collect some seeds with your feet, or build a bird blind and do some birdwatching. There are plenty of adventures waiting outside your door.

Take a hike

What better way to find out about insects in your neighbourhood than by going on an insect hike? You can find out where lacewings live, how caterpillars crawl or what earwigs eat. So, get dressed for bugwatching and let's go.

Theme hikes

How about a dragonfly hike or a grasshopper hike? If you have favourite insects, focus an outing on them. Find out what habitat they prefer and head for it. For example, dragonflies dance along the edges of ponds and streams, but grasshoppers go for long grass and wildflower meadows. When you're concentrating on only one or two kinds of insects at a time, you will be able to spend more time learning how to identify them. You can watch for features such as colour, size and wing shape and begin to recognize different species.

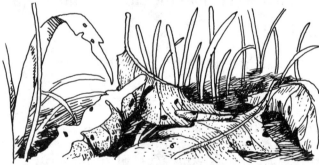

Some provinces and states have checklists for certain insects, such as butterflies, that list all the species of butterflies that have been found in a particular area. When you identify a butterfly, you can check the list to make sure the butterfly is really found in the area where you saw it. Contact your provincial or state nature organization or natural history museum to see if they have any checklists you can use.

Mini-hikes

Who said hikes have to be long, or even on foot? Take a mini-hike and give your feet a rest. Try crawling around on your hands and knees, taking time to really look at the ground for those well-hidden bugs. Or, let your fingers do the walking. Find a rotting log and probe and poke your way through it with your hands and a pair of tweezers. Take a mini-hike on a tree. Start at ground level and work your way up, checking in the grooves of bark, under loose bark, in holes, in buds, on and under leaves and in blossoms, seeds, cones or nuts. You can hike for hours and never get sore feet!

Tricks of the trade

Many insects prefer quiet, dark places and take a bit of persuasion to come into the open. Here are a few "tricks of the trade" for finding insects and luring them out into the open.

Low life
Ground-dwelling insects may come out of hiding if you tempt them with a sweet and sticky snack.

You'll need:
a trowel
a rinsed-out soup can with one end removed
a spoon
peanut butter and jam

1. In a field or woods, dig a hole big enough to hold your can. Pack soil around the can, making sure the open end is level with the ground.
2. Put a couple of spoonfuls of jam in the can and spread a thin layer of peanut butter around the inside of the rim.

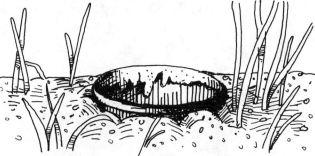

3. Leave your trap for several hours or overnight, and then come back to see what you've caught.
4. After you've had a good look at your guests, let them go. Remove your can and fill in the hole. Try placing your can in a different habitat and compare the kinds and numbers of creatures that you catch.

Shake it, baby, shake it!
Small shrubs are super hiding places for insects. Wherever they're clinging, you can shake them out to get a closer look. Take an old white or light-coloured sheet and spread it on the ground underneath a shrub. Give the bush a good shake. You should find that several different kinds of creatures have dropped on to your sheet. When you're through looking, leave them near the bottom of the bush and they will climb or fly back up.

Peek-a-boo
When out for a walk, play a game of peek-a-boo with the wildlife. Many insects and other animals shelter under stones, rocks and rotting logs. Carefully lift up these hiding places to reveal the life hiding below. If you're lucky, you'll find various beetles, ants, wood lice, centipedes, millipedes, slugs, snails, earthworms and maybe even a salamander. Don't forget to replace the stones or logs where they were so the animals will be protected.

A clean sweep

What do you see when you look at an abandoned field, unmown ditch or wild meadow? Probably a lot of tall grass and wild flowers. But it's what you don't see that's so interesting. A casual walk into the grass usually sends dozens of creatures flipping, flopping, flying and hopping in every direction. How can you get a closer look at these insects? What you need is a sweep net. You can gently catch easy-to-see and hidden insects in your net, have a good look at them and then let them go.

You'll need:
a coat hanger
wire cutters
scissors
an old, light-coloured pillowcase with a hem around the top
a needle and thread (optional)
a pocket knife
an old broom handle or hockey stick shaft
some strong, bendable wire

1. Bend the hanger into a circle. Unravel the twisted end. Ask an adult to cut off the hook with the wire cutters.

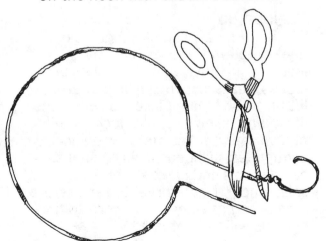

2. Cut a small opening in the hem of your pillowcase and thread your coat hanger through so that both ends stick out of the hole. The pillowcase seams should be on the inside of your net.

3. If you want a smaller net, cut some material off the closed end of the pillowcase and then sew the seam back up tightly.
4. Ask an adult to cut a deep notch, long enough for the wire ends of your hanger, on each side of the end of your broom handle.
5. Fit the hanger ends into the notches. Wrap some bendable wire tightly around the notches so that the net is held securely to the handle.

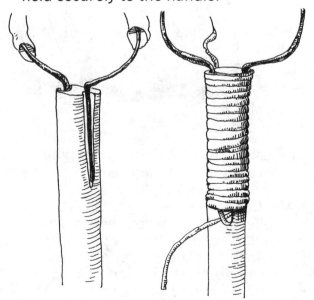

6. Drag your net back and forth through tall grass, wild flowers and low shrubs. Check your sweep net for some of these wonders. Remember — some insects will bite or sting in defence, so handle with care.

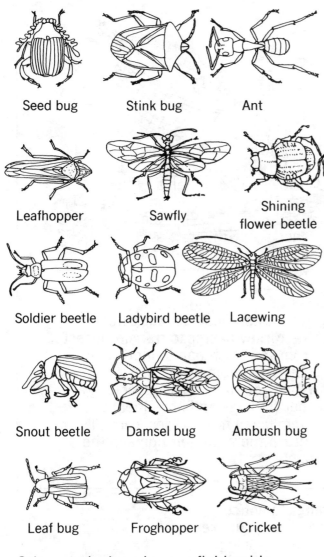

Seed bug   Stink bug   Ant

Leafhopper   Sawfly   Shining flower beetle

Soldier beetle   Ladybird beetle   Lacewing

Snout beetle   Damsel bug   Ambush bug

Leaf bug   Froghopper   Cricket

Others to look up in your field guide include treehoppers, mantids, grasshoppers, katydids, various caterpillars, aphids, shield-backed bugs and negro bugs.

I got one!

When you catch something in your net, you can get a closer look at it by carefully transferring it with tweezers into a container. Use a small, clear bottle, like a pill bottle, if the insect is small, or a large jam jar if it is big. Make sure there are air holes in the lids of your containers. To keep insects in your net from escaping while you are looking at something, simply fold the hanging part of your net up over the open end. When you've finished looking at your temporary treasures, carefully return them to where they were found.

Everything, including the kitchen sink

You've heard of fly fishing? What about fishing for flies . . . and other aquatic insects? Scrounge around the kitchen for some "tackle" and you'll be all set for one of the best fishing trips ever.

You'll need:
a shallow, light-coloured dish pan
a kitchen strainer tied to a broom handle
  for a longer reach
tweezers
a tiny paintbrush
a pail for collecting samples
a turkey baster
small, clear plastic bottles (pill bottles
  work well)
field guides to pond life, insects and
  butterflies
rubber gloves (optional—good in cold
  water)

1. Fill the dish pan with clear pond water. This will be your Home Base.
2. Dip the strainer into the pond to catch any insects swimming around. Gently jiggle your strainer around the plants, watching for any creatures that fall free.
3. Carefully transfer any finds to your Home Base using your tweezers or the paintbrush. Some insects, such as giant water bugs and water scorpions, can bite so be careful when handling all creatures.
4. Explore the mucky bottom with your strainer and pail. Scoop up a strainer full of muck and bob it up and down in the water to wash away the silt. Look for the insects left behind and transfer them to your Home Base.

5. For a closer look at your catch, use the turkey baster to transfer insects from your dish pan to individual bottles containing water.
6. When you have finished looking at your findings and have identified them using field guides, carefully return them to their home in the pond.

Things to notice
Check out your creature's . . .
- number of legs
- colour
- size
- shape
- way of travelling
- place in the pond

Make a waterscope

Have you ever stood barefoot in a pond and felt something tickling your toes or nudging your knees? Wonder what it was? Imagine that you could shrink down to fish-size and explore the underwater world. The shrinking part may be impossible, but you *can* take a peek at the underwater world using a waterscope. With a few household items you can make this watertight spy glass and start exploring.

You'll need:
a can opener (Ask an adult for help.)
a clean 1-L (1-quart) juice can
waterproof tape (packing or hockey tape is ideal)
clear plastic wrap
a large, strong elastic band
scissors

1. Using the can opener, remove both ends of the juice can. Carefully tape the sharp edges so you don't cut yourself.

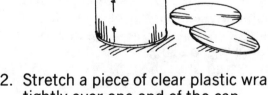

2. Stretch a piece of clear plastic wrap tightly over one end of the can, overlapping on all sides.

3. Put the elastic band around the end of the can so that the plastic wrap is held tightly in place.
4. Trim the edges of the plastic to make them even and then tape them down with the waterproof tape.

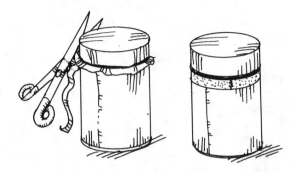

5. Test your waterscope in a basin of water. Lower the plastic-wrap end into the water, making sure that the open end never goes below the water. You look in the open end.
6. Now visit a pond or marsh and see for yourself what lurks below the water.

Have a moth ball

You don't have to dress up like a moth to attract one. In fact, with a few simple materials you can host a party for moths, and other insects, and get a good look at some of your surprising neighbours. You may want to use a field guide to help identify some of your guests.

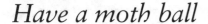

Sugaring

Just like kids, many insects love sweet stuff. You can attract moths and other insects by setting out a sweet and sticky treat. Moths are more easily attracted at dusk, but you can use the same bait and method for attracting other insects during the day.

You'll need:
sugar or molasses
stale fruit juice
spoiled, mashed up fruit (bananas work
  well)
a bowl and spoon
trees
an old paintbrush
a flashlight

1. Mix up the sugar, juice and fruit in a bowl.
2. Late in the day choose a tree, or trees, and use an old paintbrush to paint the mixture on the trunk.
3. Return about an hour later in the dark. Use your flashlight to see who's dropped in.
4. You can make a moth trail by painting several trees along a route that can be walked in 20-30 minutes. Try to end up where you started. By the time the last tree has been painted, some insects may already be at the first tree. Follow the route around, checking to see what has been attracted at each stop.

Light lovers

Have you ever noticed all the insects flying around street lights at night? Lights are often used to attract insects that fly in the evening, especially moths. Areas with lots of trees and flowers — like backyards, parks or woods — are good places to watch night fliers.

You'll need:

tacks
an old white sheet
a light (porch light, large flashlight or lantern)
a large glass jar and lid with holes punched in
a plant stem or twig to put inside the jar

1. Tack the sheet on the side of a building or from the branch of a tree.
2. Shine a bright light on the sheet at night.
3. You can stand very close to the sheet without scaring off the insects. When an insect lands on the sheet, try to catch it in your jar for a closer look. Let it go when you are finished.

Insect-eating plants

If you like science fiction, you've probably read about incredible flesh-eating plants that terrorize people and animals. But did you know that about 450 different kinds of meat-eating (carnivorous) plants really exist? They don't attack people, of course, but they do trap and digest a variety of tiny insects for food.

Clamming up
Venus fly traps are famous everywhere but actually only grow in North and South Carolina in the United States. Their hinged leaves are fringed with long bristles that are very sensitive to touch. When disturbed, the leaf snaps shut, like a clam, trapping its prey inside.

Trap doors
Bladderwort uses a tricky trapdoor to catch unsuspecting insects. It grows in the water of ponds and ditches and has pouch-like bladders that are attached to floating leaves. The bladders are fringed with hairs, so when an insect touches the hairs, a trapdoor swings open, the bladder inflates and the prey is sucked inside.

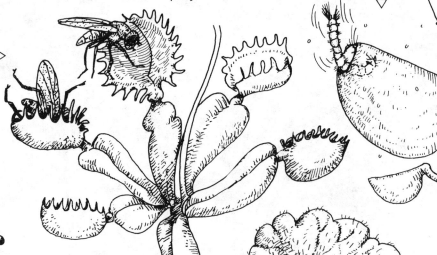

Sticky stuff
Sundews may be small, but they're tough on insects. This bog plant gets its name because of its leaves' long hairs, tipped with drops of sticky moisture. Insects get stuck to the glue-like substance on the hairs. Then the leaves fold over to enclose the insect in a sort of temporary stomach.

In the drink
If you were an insect, you wouldn't want to stop for a drink from the pitcher plant. It attracts insects to its liquid-filled pitchers and then downward-pointing hairs prevent the insects from escaping. Once in the jug, the prey drowns and is soon digested.

Be a pitcher plant

You can catch an insect the same way a pitcher plant does, but instead of eating your catch, just have a close look at it before letting it go.

You'll need:
a plastic funnel
a sharp knife
a piece of juicy fruit or fruit juice
a wide-mouth jar

1. Ask an adult to cut off the narrow part of the funnel so that the opening is about 1 cm (½ inch) across.
2. Rub the piece of fruit over the inside of the funnel or pour some fruit juice on it so that the funnel is sticky and sweet smelling.
3. Place the fruit in the bottom of the jar.
4. Set the funnel in the mouth of the jar with the narrow part of the funnel pointing down.
5. Place your jar outside in an open area, like a field or backyard, and wait for your first visitor. Watch what happens when a fly or wasp lands on the funnel. The fruit will attract it down the funnel into the jar below, just as a pitcher plant attracts its prey. Once inside the jar, the insect will not be able to get out until you take the funnel away.

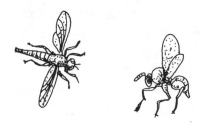

Peek into a plant

Have you ever seen a goldenrod plant with a round or egg-shaped lump on its stem? These odd shapes, called galls, are not natural parts of the plant. They are caused by a fly or moth that moves in for the winter. Goldenrod galls are one of the most common galls, but many different types exist in buds, leaves, flowers, stems, twigs and even in roots of flowers, shrubs and trees.

The inside story

Goldenrod galls are formed when an adult insect lays an egg on the surface of the plant's stem. When the egg hatches, the larva (a fat, white grub) crawls along the stem, bores a hole and then crawls in. Not surprisingly, this invasion bothers the plant and it responds to the "irritation" by making extra thick layers of plant tissue around the grub. These extra layers form the gall.

Inside the gall, the larva is in insect heaven. It's surrounded by food (the plant itself), it's safe from the winter's cold and it's hidden from many predators. Living in a gall is like having a refrigerator in your cosy bedroom. Most gall insects spend winter as larvae and then change

into pupae in early spring. By early summer, a tiny adult fly or moth emerges from a little hole in the gall, completing the life cycle.

Good gall-y!
There are more than 1500 gall-making insects in North America. Even though plants and trees have no use for galls, people do. In the past, people boiled galls to extract their pigments (natural colours). These colours were used for dying wool, skin, hair and leather. Tannic acid, used in tanning and ink making, also comes from insect galls.

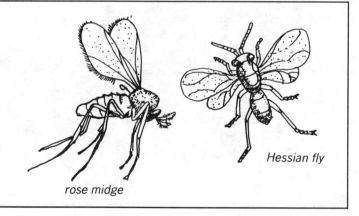

rose midge

Hessian fly

Gall collecting

Galls are fascinating mini-habitats for tiny insects and are easy to collect.

You'll need:
scissors
a bag
a pen knife
jars
screening or cheesecloth
elastic bands

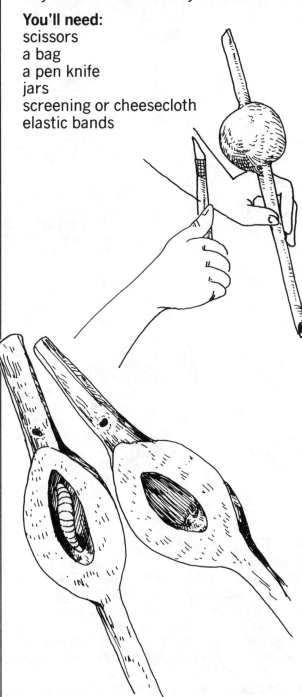

1. In late summer, fall or winter, take a walk through a patch of goldenrod and collect several large round and egg-shaped galls. Use scissors to cut the stems. Place your galls in a bag. Try collecting many different galls to compare their size, shape and makers. Galls are also commonly found on oak, poplar and willow trees.

2. At home, open up a few of your galls. Ask an adult to cut them open with a sharp knife. Be careful not to damage the grub inside. If the gall is empty, look for escape holes. The gall may have been abandoned earlier in the year, or a hungry chickadee or Downy Woodpecker may have beaten you to the larva. Sometimes you'll find an unexpected resident in the gall. It may be a parasite that has killed the gall maker or a spider, bee, ant, beetle or thrip that has just moved into the empty gall.

3. Place an uncut sample of each kind of gall in jars covered with screening or with cheesecloth, tied with elastic bands.

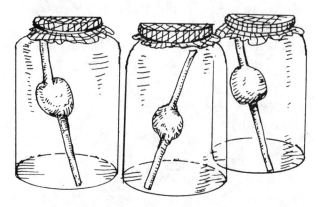

4. Put your jars in an unheated area, such as the garage or balcony, and leave them for several months. In late spring, watch for the emergence of the tiny adult insects.

Look for life on a leaf

The next time you jump into a pile of leaves, take a closer look at what you've landed in. If there are oak, poplar, birch or fruit tree leaves in your pile, you're in for a surprise. Your leaves provide food and homes for a variety of tiny insects. Here are a few things to look for.

Leaf miners
If your leaf has small see-through blotches in it, like tiny windows, or a winding maze of trails, it has probably been invaded by leaf miners. The larvae of leaf-mining flies, beetles, wasps, butterflies and moths are so tiny that they can burrow into the space between the upper and lower surfaces of a leaf. They eat the soft leaf tissue (the green part) and leave the stringy bits behind. Insects that wander while they eat create a system of tiny pathways that show you where they've been.

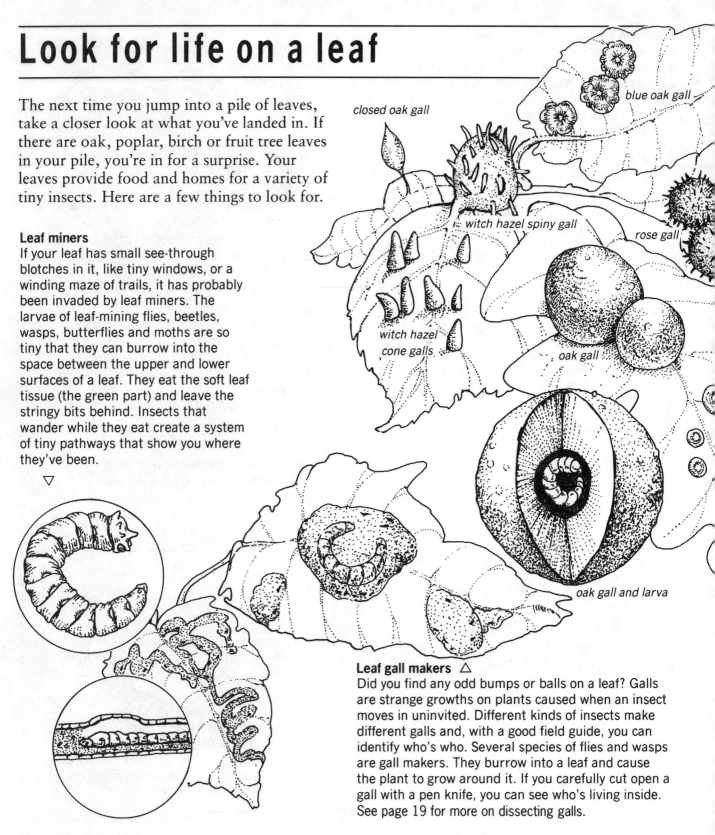

closed oak gall

blue oak gall

witch hazel spiny gall

rose gall

witch hazel cone galls

oak gall

oak gall and larva

Leaf gall makers △
Did you find any odd bumps or balls on a leaf? Galls are strange growths on plants caused when an insect moves in uninvited. Different kinds of insects make different galls and, with a good field guide, you can identify who's who. Several species of flies and wasps are gall makers. They burrow into a leaf and cause the plant to grow around it. If you carefully cut open a gall with a pen knife, you can see who's living inside. See page 19 for more on dissecting galls.

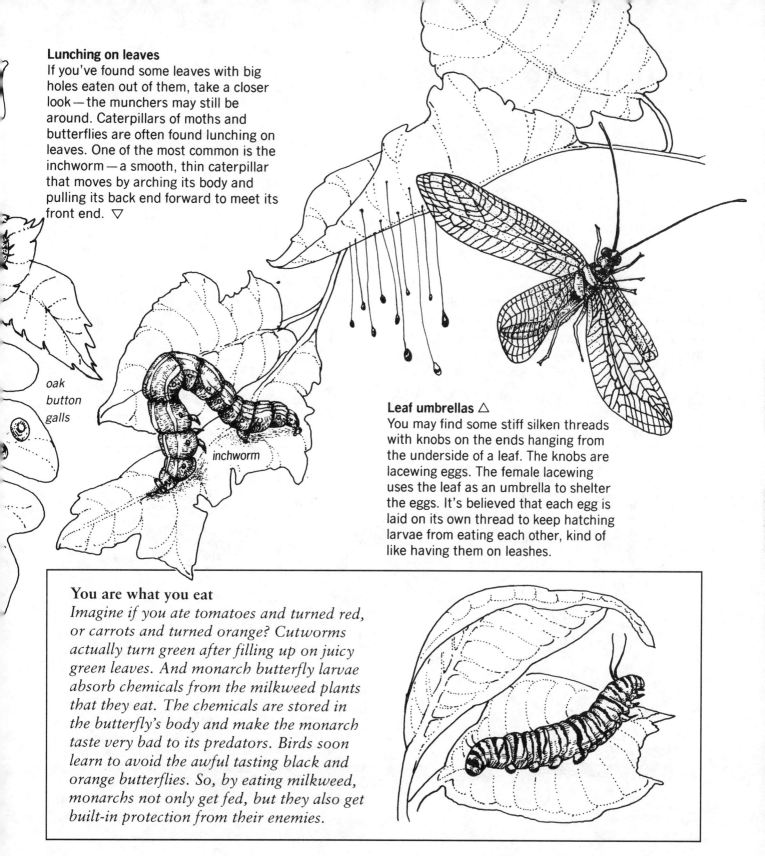

Lunching on leaves

If you've found some leaves with big holes eaten out of them, take a closer look—the munchers may still be around. Caterpillars of moths and butterflies are often found lunching on leaves. One of the most common is the inchworm—a smooth, thin caterpillar that moves by arching its body and pulling its back end forward to meet its front end. ▽

oak
button
galls

inchworm

Leaf umbrellas △

You may find some stiff silken threads with knobs on the ends hanging from the underside of a leaf. The knobs are lacewing eggs. The female lacewing uses the leaf as an umbrella to shelter the eggs. It's believed that each egg is laid on its own thread to keep hatching larvae from eating each other, kind of like having them on leashes.

You are what you eat

Imagine if you ate tomatoes and turned red, or carrots and turned orange? Cutworms actually turn green after filling up on juicy green leaves. And monarch butterfly larvae absorb chemicals from the milkweed plants that they eat. The chemicals are stored in the butterfly's body and make the monarch taste very bad to its predators. Birds soon learn to avoid the awful tasting black and orange butterflies. So, by eating milkweed, monarchs not only get fed, but they also get built-in protection from their enemies.

Looking at leaves

Your hand is like a leaf. Look at the underside of your wrist and notice all the veins running from your arm into your hand. Leaves also have veins that run from the branch into the leaves. The veins in your hand are covered by skin and tissue and are hard to see. Although a leaf's veins are covered by leaf tissue, their outlines are visible as ridges on the leaf. Your veins carry blood from your hand back to your heart. Plants don't have blood, of course, but they do have a watery liquid called sap in their veins. Inside the veins of a leaf are two sets of tubes. One set of tubes, called xylem (zi-lem), carries water and minerals from the roots into the leaves. The other set of tubes, called

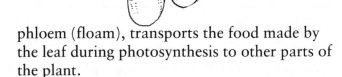

phloem (floam), transports the food made by the leaf during photosynthesis to other parts of the plant.

The veins also act like bones. They provide support to the leaf tissue, like your bones support your body's tissues. When there is a lot of water available to the plant, the veins are full of sap and the leaves are well supported. But if water is not available, the veins will lose their stiffness and the leaf will collapse, or wilt. To get a closer look at a leaf's veins and compare the vein patterns of different kinds of leaves, you can strip away the tissue and make leaf skeletons (see page 24).

Collecting leaves

Take a look at the leaves in your garden, in your local park or on your houseplants. What kinds of shapes do you see? There's an almost endless variety of plant leaves, and that makes looking at them and collecting them lots of fun. Here's an easy way to preserve the leaves in your collection.

You'll need:
a variety of leaf shapes
waxed paper
a dish towel
an iron (Ask an adult to help you.)
glue
several sheets of three-ring binder paper
a binder

1. Collect a sampling of undamaged leaves from a variety of plants. Try to find as many different shapes as possible. You can collect green leaves in summer and coloured leaves in fall.

2. Fold a piece of waxed paper in half so that the waxy surface is on the inside. Make sure the folded paper is large enough to cover your biggest leaf.

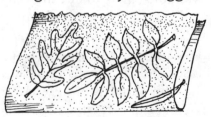

3. Place a leaf between the folded waxed paper. Cover the paper with a dish towel and carefully iron on top with a hot iron. The heat from the iron will melt the wax onto the leaf. This waxing process should prevent the leaf from drying out.

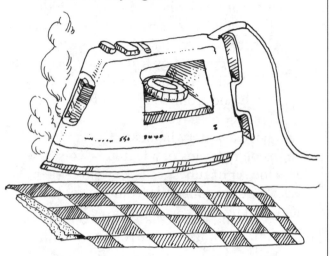

4. Glue each leaf to a sheet of paper. Beside the leaf, write where you found it, when, and what kind it is.

sugar maple
backyard October

5. Store your collection in a binder.

Making leaf skeletons

With some water and warm weather, you can get an undercover look at the leaves in your neighbourhood.

You'll need:
a variety of green leaves (maple, poplar, elm, basswood)
a dishpan
water
garden soil or compost (not sterilized soil)
old newspapers
a bowl
paper towels
paint (optional)
glue (optional)
heavy paper (optional)

1. Place the leaves flat in the bottom of your dishpan and cover them with water. Add some soil to the water. Bacteria in the soil will help the leaf tissue decompose.
2. Put newspapers on top to weigh down the leaves.

3. Leave the dishpan outside in a sunny spot for two to three weeks. The water-leaf mixture may begin to smell as the leaf tissue rots, so it is best to leave it undisturbed and away from the house.

4. Remove the newspapers and take out a few leaves at a time.
5. Place the leaves in a bowl of warm water and very gently rub them between your thumb and forefinger. This should remove the remaining leaf tissue and expose the veins.

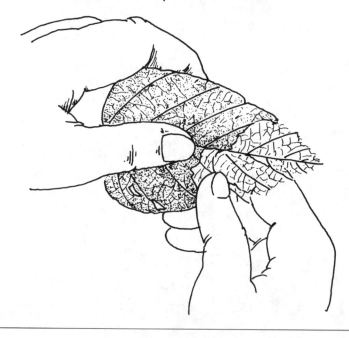

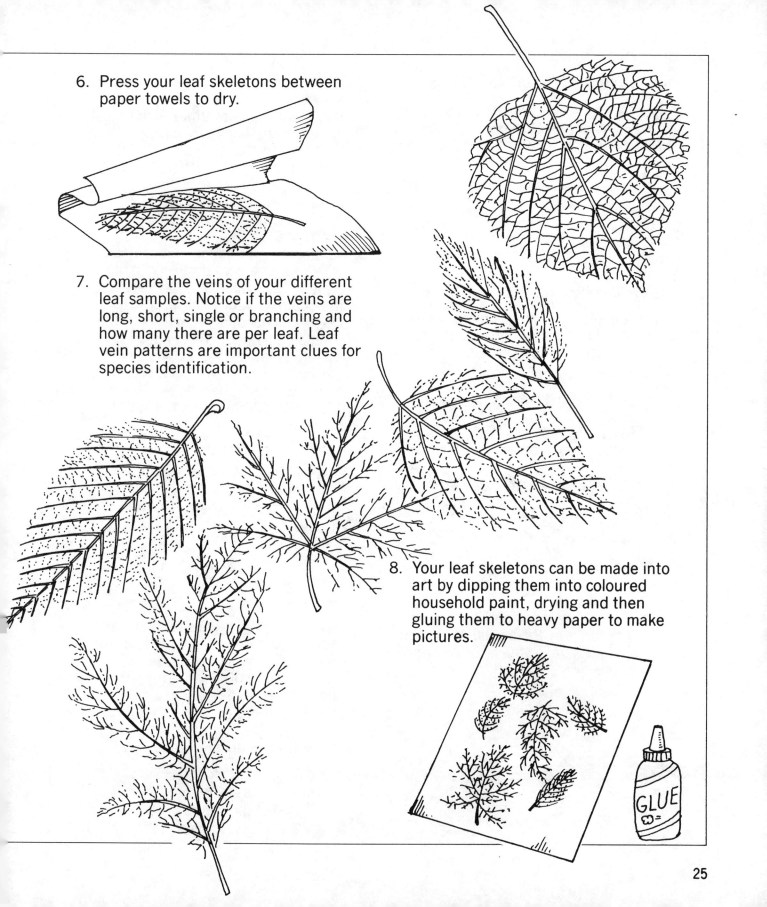

6. Press your leaf skeletons between paper towels to dry.

7. Compare the veins of your different leaf samples. Notice if the veins are long, short, single or branching and how many there are per leaf. Leaf vein patterns are important clues for species identification.

8. Your leaf skeletons can be made into art by dipping them into coloured household paint, drying and then gluing them to heavy paper to make pictures.

GLUE

Socking it to seeds

You can get a great collection of seeds by letting your feet do all the work. Here's how.

You'll need:
a pair of old wool socks
tweezers
glue
heavy paper
labels
a pen
small clear bottles with lids

1. Put the old wool socks on over your shoes and take a walk through a field in late summer or early fall.

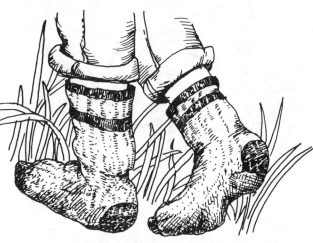

2. You'll find that a variety of seeds will be picked up by the socks. At the end of your walk, take your socks off and use tweezers to pick off the seeds.

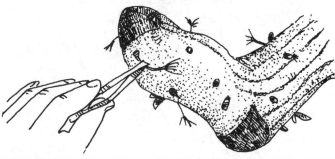

3. Try to separate the seeds by size, shape or colour. How many different kinds did you get? What is the most common seed in your collection? What might this tell you about the plants growing in the field?
4. You can try the same activity in a forest or across a backyard and compare the number and variety of seeds you get.
5. To display your collection, you can glue your seeds in groups to heavy paper. Your collection may represent the seeds of your backyard or neighbourhood, a particular habitat such as a field, or the seeds may be sorted by shape, size, colour, or method of dispersal. Each group of seeds should be labelled, saying when and where it was found.

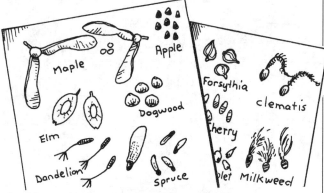

6. You may want to keep some of your seeds in bottles over the winter and plant them the following spring to see what kind of plants they grow into. Store these seeds in an unheated place or in the refrigerator to simulate the natural cold that seeds endure during winter outdoors.

Scores of spores

Like mushrooms, ferns reproduce by microscopic spores. When a fern is three to seven years old, spores form in tiny spore cases, often on the backs of the fern's fronds. When they're ripe, the spore cases burst, releasing the dust-like spores to the wind. A single plant may produce as many as 50 million spores in one season. Some can travel as far as 15 000 km (10 000 miles) away from the parent plant.

You can search for spores on different ferns. The colour of the spore cases, shape and location of the spores are important clues to a fern's identity.

You'll need:
different ferns
a magnifying glass
a field guide to ferns

1. The spore cases are often arranged in tiny, dot-like masses, called fruit-dots. Use your magnifying glass to check the underside of the fern frond for fruit-dots. What colour are they? They should be either yellow, orange or brown.

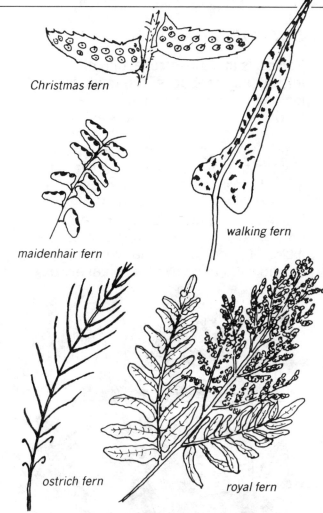

Christmas fern

maidenhair fern

walking fern

ostrich fern

royal fern

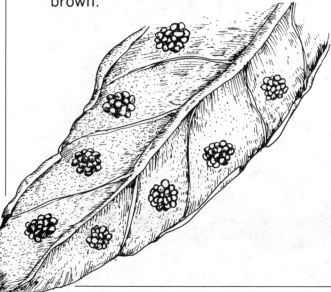

2. Notice how the fruit-dots are arranged on the frond. In some ferns, they are laid out in a definite pattern along the back of the frond (Christmas fern), while in others they are along the edge of the leaflets (maidenhair fern). The walking fern appears to have its fruit-dots scattered randomly over the fronds.
3. If there are no fruit-dots visible on the fronds, the spore cases may be growing on a special part of the frond (interrupted fern or royal fern), or even on separate stalks (cinnamon fern or ostrich fern).

Hike a tree

Nature is like a big trunk full of interesting treasures. You may start out looking for one particular thing and before you know it, you've spent hours examining all of the other contents of the trunk. You may even forget what you started to look for! When you set out to look at a tree's bark or leaves, you can end up discovering amazing things about the insects, spiders, birds and other animals that live in or on the tree. To get a close-up look at your favourite tree and see how it's used by others, take a tree hike.

You'll need:
a magnifying glass
a trowel

1. Explore your tree from the ground up. Use your trowel to gently dig around the base of the tree. You may get a look at some of the tree's surface roots and, if you're lucky, you'll uncover some root-feeding insects such as cicada nymphs. Loose bark near the base of the tree is also a good hiding place for spiders and cocoons.

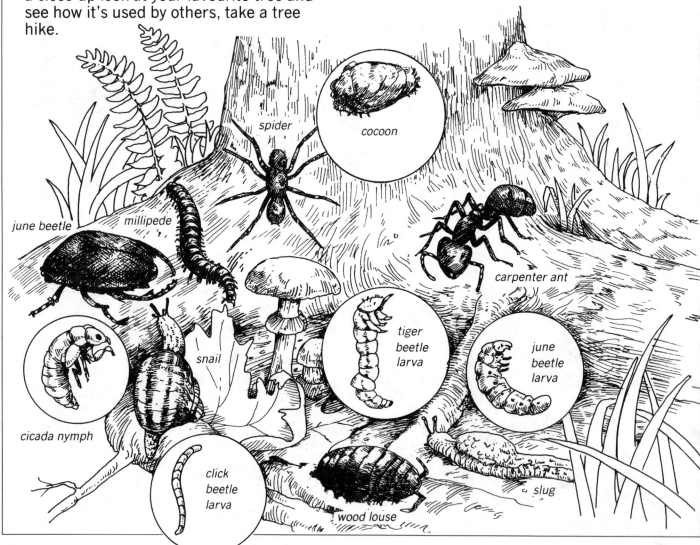

spider

cocoon

june beetle

millipede

carpenter ant

cicada nymph

snail

tiger beetle larva

june beetle larva

click beetle larva

wood louse

slug

2. Scan the cracks and crevices of the bark for insects and other invertebrates. Some spiders make tube-shaped webs on bark, while engraver beetles and carpenter ants leave entrance holes. And speaking of holes, check for the tell-tale signs of woodpeckers and sapsuckers. You may find mosses and lichens growing on the bark.

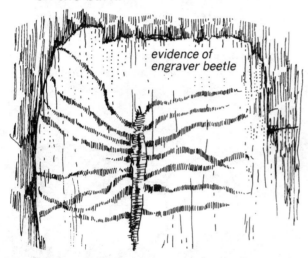

evidence of engraver beetle

3. Leaves provide homes to all kinds of creatures. Look for knobby growths caused by insect galls or fungi. Tiny transparent tunnels across a leaf are the signs of leaf miners. Unroll any cigar-shaped leaves to see if the young insects are still at home.

4. Look up. Are there any nests up in the branches? You may also see caches of food left by squirrels or birds in the crotches of large branches.

5. Depending on the time of year, you can check out the tree's buds, flowers or cones, too.

Tree totalling

If you grew like most trees do, the older you became, the fatter you'd grow. A tree trunk grows in width each year in a microscopically thin layer called the cambium. Towards the outside of the tree, the cambium produces phloem (floam) cells under the bark. These cells carry food up and down the tree until they die and form part of the bark. On the inside of the tree, the cambium divides into xylem cells that pipe water and minerals to the leaves, store food and form the support of the tree. In the spring or wet season, the growing conditions are usually best and large cells are produced, forming a wide, light-coloured ring of relatively soft wood inside the tree. In the summer or dry season, however, smaller, more condensed, thick-walled cells are formed, creating a dark ring of harder wood. The combination of one light and one dark ring represents one year's growth.

When a tree trunk is cut across its diameter, you can easily see the fresh rings. By starting at the centre and counting each pair of light and dark rings, you can tell how old the tree is. How old is the tree illustrated here? (Answer on page 158.)

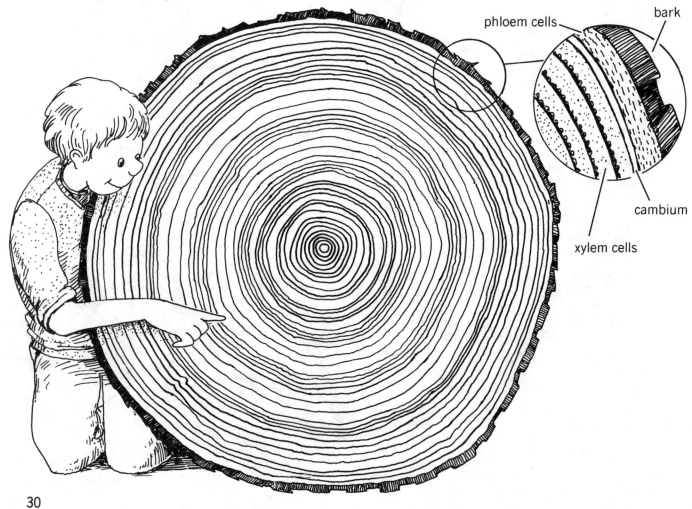

phloem cells

bark

cambium

xylem cells

Diary of a tree

You can find out more than just a tree's age from looking at its rings; you can also see what kind of life it's had.

Depending on the width of a ring, you can tell whether or not it was a good year for growth. For example, a very narrow, light-coloured ring may indicate that the tree suffered from a drought or too much shading from other trees for proper growth. Fire scars can be visible as charred areas, and signs of insect damage or disease may also be present. Sugar maple trees that have been tapped through the years may show the scars where the spiles were inserted. It's like reading a tree's diary of past events.

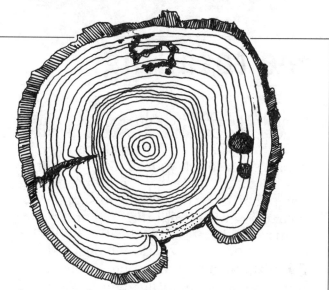

Branching out

Instead of looking on the inside of a pine tree to estimate how old it is, you can do it from the outside. Each year a pine tree adds a new whorl, or circle of branches, around its trunk. You can count the number of whorls to figure out how old the tree is. How old do you think this pine tree is? Turn to page 158 to see if you are right.

How high is up?

Trees are the tallest of all living things, and the Californian redwood is the tallest species of plant alive. Its record height is more than 63 times the height of the average person. If you want to find out the height of the tallest trees in your neighbourhood, try these two simple measuring tricks with the help of a friend.

Eyeballing it

You'll need:
a friend
a measuring stick
a pencil
paper

1. Stand facing the tree you want to measure. Hold your arm straight out in front of you so that your fist is level with your eye. Ask a friend to measure and record the distance between your eye and your fist (distance 1 on the diagram).
2. Hold a measuring stick straight up and down in your hand so that the distance from your hand to the top of the stick equals distance 1. (This is labelled 2 on the diagram; distance 1 = distance 2.)
3. Keeping your arm outstretched and your fist at eye level, walk backwards from the tree. Stop when the base of the tree lines up with the top of your fist and the highest twig of the tree lines up with the top of your stick.
4. Ask a friend to measure the distance between you and the tree trunk (labelled distance 3 on the diagram). This distance equals the height of your tree.

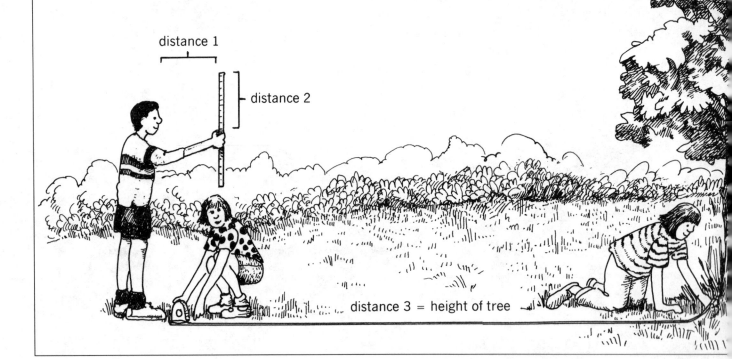

distance 1

distance 2

distance 3 = height of tree

Casting Shadows

You'll need:
a measuring stick or tape
a pencil
paper
a friend

1. On a sunny day, find a tree in an open area where its shadow is visible on the ground.
2. Measure and record your friend's height.
3. Have your friend stand near the tree, so that his shadow falls alongside the tree's shadow. Measure and record the length of your friend's shadow and the tree's shadow. Make sure all your measurements are in the same units (e.g., all in metres or centimetres).
4. Calculate the tree's height using this formula:

$$\text{tree's height} = \frac{\text{length of tree's shadow} \times \text{friend's height}}{\text{length of friend's shadow}}$$

Check the example below to see if you're doing your calculations correctly.

$$\text{tree's height} = \frac{\text{tree's shadow} \times \text{friend's height}}{\text{friend's shadow (3 m)}} \frac{(20\text{ m}) \quad (1.5\text{ m})}{}$$

$$\text{tree's height} = \frac{30\text{ m}}{3\text{ m}}$$

$$\text{tree's height} = 10\text{ m}$$

Beginner birdwatching

If you were asked to describe yourself, you might say, "Short, brown hair, blue eyes, freckles, skinny with big feet." This physical description would help a stranger identify you. Birdwatchers also use physical descriptions to help them identify birds.

Name dropping

You may like the idea of being able to see a bird and know its name. The more you birdwatch, the more names you will learn and remember. However, knowing a bird's name is not the most important thing in birdwatching. There are many other ways to identify a bird— by the type of habitat it lives in, what it eats, how it looks or what it is doing. For example, if you can see a bird and recognize it as an insect-eater because it has a narrow, pointed beak, then you are well on your way to becoming a birdwatcher.

When you see a bird . . .

□ Try to estimate the **size** of the bird. Is it closest in size to a sparrow, a robin or a crow?

Robin

Crow

Sparrow

□ Describe the bird's body **shape.** Is it plump like a robin or slender?

Mockingbird

Robin

□ Sometimes different **body parts** stand out as easy identification features. Ask yourself the following questions:
—Does the bird have a crest on its head?
—Are its legs long or short?
—Is its tail forked, squared, pointed or cocked up?

Pigeon

House Wren

Barn Swallow

—Does it have a thick beak, a small, pointed beak or a very long, dagger-shaped beak?

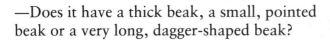

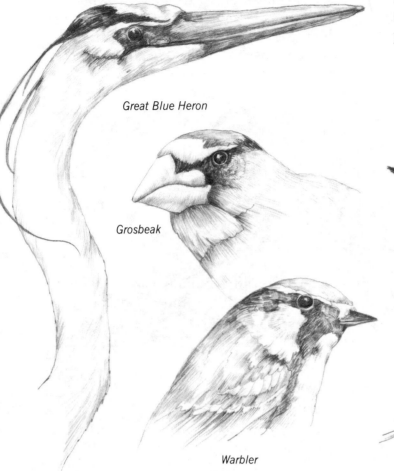

Great Blue Heron

Grosbeak

Warbler

□ Some birds have **special colouring or markings** that make them easier to remember. Look for eye stripes, speckled or streaked breasts, wingbars, tail stripes and patches of colour.

Hooded Warbler

Western Meadowlark

American Goldfinch

□ How a bird **moves** can be an important clue to its identity. For instance, the roller-coaster flight of the American Goldfinch helps you identify it at a distance. Take note of where the bird is and what it is doing.

—In the water, is it wading or diving?

—In the air, is it flying straight or up and down? Is it swooping, circling, gliding or hovering?

—On the ground, is it hopping, walking or bobbing?

—On a tree, is it hopping up the bark, climbing down headfirst or climbing up in a spiral pattern?

The bird's **location** can help you identify it. For instance, you're not likely to find a Mallard Duck in a forest or a Great Blue Heron in a dry meadow. They're more likely to be found by a lake. In addition to habitat, the country, state or province where you see a bird is important. All birds have a particular range where you can expect to see them. Some birds have a huge range covering most of North America, while others may be found in certain areas. If you think you have identified a specific bird, check a range map in a field guide just to make sure it actually lives there.

Eastern Meadowlark and range

Look around

You can hear it, but you can't see it. Sound familiar? Some birds are so well hidden that it may take a lot of patience and persistence on your part to find them. Don't forget to look at tree branches, tree trunks, tree tops, fallen logs, rocks, the ground, flower or grass stalks in a field or garden, shoreline or marsh vegetation and hedgerows. Try "spishing." This is a noise you can make, almost like whispering to a friend (*psst*), which can encourage a bird to come out into the open.

When birdwatching, visit as many different habitats as possible, such as a meadow, wood, marsh, lake, ocean, cliff, desert or beach.

Dressing for birdwatching

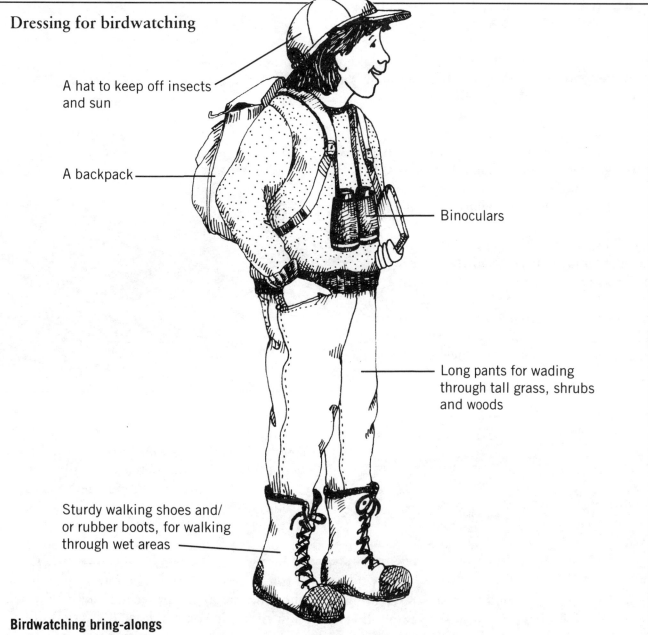

A hat to keep off insects and sun

A backpack

Binoculars

Long pants for wading through tall grass, shrubs and woods

Sturdy walking shoes and/or rubber boots, for walking through wet areas

Birdwatching bring-alongs

You don't need much, but these items can help make your birdwatching more successful.

- *lunch or snacks for you*
- *a snack for the birds. Chickadees, for example, can be encouraged to feed out of your hand.*

- *a field guide to birds*
- *a bird checklist (many provinces, states and parks have these for visitors)*
- *a pencil*
- *insect repellent (depending on time of year)*

Nest watching

Nests are like the birds that build them. They come in a variety of sizes and shapes. For example, the largest known bird's nest in North America belonged to a Florida Bald Eagle. It weighed the same as two compact cars and it was bigger than a hot tub. At the other end of the scale is the tiny nest of the Ruby-throated Hummingbird. It's smaller than an egg cup.

What are nests made of? Sticks, mosses, lichens, grasses, mud, feathers, bark, straw and rootlets are popular nest-building materials. But some birds such as hummingbirds, some warblers, bushtits and Blue-gray Gnatcatchers even steal spider silk and use it to reinforce their nests.

A hummingbird nest, actual size

An eagle's nest

Weaverbird nest

Watching a bird build a nest is fascinating. Some birds work with painstaking care; others just slap their nests together. Often it's the female that builds the nest, but sometimes the male will help out. A dramatic example of nest-building skill is found in the weaverbirds of Africa, India and Australia. They actually weave grass into a basket-like nest, just like a person might weave a basket. Could it be that ancient people learned how to make baskets by watching weaverbirds?

Be careful!

You can learn a lot about birds by watching them build a nest and take care of their eggs. One of the first things you must learn is to be careful.

Great care must be taken not to disturb the nest or the young. Parents may be frightened off by too much attention, leaving their young to starve. Some parents become very angry when their nest is approached and will attack an intruder. In some places "BEWARE OF BIRD" signs have to be posted to keep people away from nests and protective parents. Watching from a bird blind is a good way to make sure you don't disturb parents and young. See page 42 for information on how to build one. If you're careful, you can watch a nest over the entire breeding period and see as the young hatch, grow, learn to fly and fledge (leave the nest on their own).

Take note

To help you compare the family life of different species and help you remember some of the details of your hours spent nest-watching, keep a daily journal of your observations describing the activities at the nest. You can make notes on feeding habits, daily routines, changes in appearance of the young and many other interesting features. If you have a camera, some photographs of the nest and young at different stages of development would provide wonderful highlights to your diary.

A year-round hobby

After the breeding season is over, you can look for nests. They are especially easy to spot if you live in an area where the trees lose their leaves in autumn. An abandoned nest can provide you with a chance to get a really close-up view of how the nest is constructed. In addition, you may be able to identify the nest's owners using a field guide to bird nests. Even though they are no longer being used by the owners, these nests should not be removed. Sometimes old nests are used as shelter later in the year by other species. In some cases, nests are reused by their owners for several years, or the abandoned nest of one bird may be taken over by a different bird the following year.

Nests to notice

Here are some neat nests to get you started on a nest-watching hobby.

A make-do nest

The Cliff Swallow builds an unusual gourd-shaped nest with a narrow side entrance leading to an enlarged chamber. If no cliff is available, the nest is tucked under the eaves of a barn or other building. In a barn, local materials are used — straw, mud and even horsehair!

Nest, sweet nest

The Osprey builds a large cup-shaped nest of sticks, twigs, driftwood and weed stalks and lines it with grass, algae or feathers. Although they are usually built in a treetop near water, Osprey nests are also found on buildings and hydro poles. The Osprey often uses the same nest year after year, renovating and enlarging it each year.

Underground nest

The male and female Belted Kingfishers deserve a medal for nest engineering. They dig a burrow as long as a canoe paddle in a steep river or pond bank and lay their eggs on the bare floor of a circular chamber at the end of the burrow. As feeding occurs, fish bones pile up on the floor, providing the young with a prickly mattress.

Secret entrance

The Marsh Wren weaves grasses and reed stalks into a ball-shaped nest and lines it with finer grasses, cat-tail down and feathers. Found in cat-tail marshes, these small nests have a clever side entrance that helps to hide the eggs and young from predators flying overhead. Although the eggs are laid in only one nest, male Marsh Wrens build several nests to fool their enemies.

Tree nest

The Hairy Woodpecker drills a gourd-shaped nesting cavity into live trees, sometimes in maple swamps or apple orchards. It doesn't bother to build a nest in the cavity; it just lines the hole with wood chips.

How not to be seen

The most successful birdwatchers are the quietest and best-hidden ones. Like other animals, birds are easily frightened, especially during breeding season. The best way to avoid problems and get the best seat in the house is to make yourself invisible—or close to it! Building a bird blind and dressing to disappear are two good ways to hide from birds.

Seeing blinds

Bird blinds are small enclosures that hide you from the animal you are watching. A photographer will often use a blind to take pictures of wildlife in their natural habitat without scaring them away. There are many different kinds of blinds: some are built on land, others float on water and still others are built up in trees. They may be constructed from natural materials, such as a thick mass of cat-tails cut off and stuck in the mud around you in a marsh, or built by covering a frame with canvas or burlap. The simple blinds you see here will increase your chances of seeing birds close up.

Visit an area for a few days before putting up your blind so you will know the best place for it and the best time of day to use it. Even when you are out of sight, wildlife may not appear right away. Patience is very important because wild animals do not give "command performances." Make the blind large enough to allow you to sit comfortably. In addition to your binoculars, field guide and possibly a journal for taking notes, bring along something quiet to pass the time, such as food, a book or a puzzle. Your time and effort will be rewarded when you get close to wildlife, see them in their own homes and find out some of the fascinating secrets of their lives.

A body blind

You don't need to build or grow a fancy blind to hide from the birds. Try dressing in camouflage colours—greens and browns—so that you blend in with the background. Wear a hat, a long-sleeved shirt and long pants. This get-up will not only camouflage you so that you don't frighten off nervous birds; it'll also protect you from insect bites while you watch the wildlife.

Umbrella blind

Rain or shine, you can use this collapsible blind just about anywhere.

You'll need: a hammer
a stake or hollow aluminum pole
an umbrella (not a bright colour)
60 cm (2 feet) of bendable wire
safety pins
canvas or burlap (preferably
brown or green)
heavy stones
scissors

1. Hammer your stake or pole into the ground in the centre of your site.
2. Using wire, attach the handle of an umbrella to the pole.
3. Using safety pins, fasten the cloth to the umbrella so that it extends right down to the ground on all sides to create a tent-like enclosure.
4. Weigh down the edges of the material with heavy stones.
5. Cut viewing holes at your eye-level all around the blind so you can see out in all directions.

A living blind

Grow your own blind and hide from the birds while adding pretty flowers to your garden.

You'll need: 1.2 m (4 feet) of binder twine
4 poles, 1.5-1.8 m (5-6 feet)
high
a shovel
runner bean or morning glory
seeds
string
cedar or pine boughs (optional)

1. Use the binder twine to lash your poles together in a teepee style.
2. Dig up a narrow strip of earth around the base of your blind for planting.
3. Plant the morning glory or runner bean seeds around three sides of your blind and care for them according to the directions on the package.

4. When the vines grow, tie them to your frame with string so that they grow up the poles. Not only will you have pretty flowers on your blind, but hummingbirds and butterflies may also visit the blossoms, giving you a really close-up view.
5. If you live in an area where planting vines is not possible, tie cedar or pine boughs to the frame instead.

Pretty as a picture

Why not try combining two great hobbies: birdwatching and photography? That way you can record your birding triumphs on film and keep them as lasting memories. Although professionals use complex and expensive camera equipment, with practice you can get a lot of pleasure from a simple camera.

Candid camera

Many of your birdwatching skills can be applied to photography. For instance, being quiet and well hidden is very important not only so a bird will come close enough for a good picture, but also so that it will act naturally. You can hide yourself and your camera behind bushes or rocks. Or you can build a bird blind (see page 42). A blind is especially useful for photographing nesting birds without disturbing them. You can even stay in your house and take a photograph through an open window. If you are using a camera that gives you pictures instantly, your subject should be within a few feet for a really good picture. Experiment with some photos to get an idea of what distance is best.

Setting up

Backyards or local parks are good places to develop your skills. Choose an area with a nice background for a photo. For instance, berry-covered shrubs, a flower bed or an old stump will be much nicer than a clothesline, driveway or other non-natural feature. Once you have a location, try to attract birds to it by putting out bird seed or a bird bath. If you're using a blind, set it up so that you will have a good view of where the birds might land.

Picture this

One picture of a bird may show something about the bird's appearance or behaviour, but a series of pictures can tell a whole story. If you are watching a nest over a period of several days or weeks, take pictures often. When laid out in sequence, your pictures will show the bird's story from egg to fledgling.

You can also concentrate on one species of bird, say a robin. Photograph robins as they do different things such as perching, walking, flying, poking for worms, eating fruit or bathing. Put your pictures together in a story-like format to show others what a robin's life is like.

Lighten up

Lighting is an important part of your picture. When using a simple camera, make sure your subject is well lit, but do not point your camera into the sun when photographing. Try to ensure some contrast in your picture. For example, a dark-coloured bird will show up much better against a light-coloured background such as snow or sky than against a dark tree trunk or forest floor.

Sketching birds

You can take birdwatching one step further by sketching the birds you see. Because birds in the wild tend to move around a lot, or are well hidden, they can be difficult for a beginner to sketch. When starting out, use photographs or magazine pictures of birds or visit a museum and sketch the stuffed birds on display. Once you master the basic skills of sketching, you can move on to the birds outdoors.

You'll need: a soft pencil—B, 2B, 3B (No. 2)
     or softer
     a pad of blank paper
     a hard surface, such as a
      clipboard, to work on
     photographs or pictures from bird
      magazines (optional)

Shaping up

Look at the basic outline of the bird illustrated here. Do any of the body parts remind you of basic shapes? All birds have oval bodies. It is what's attached to the bodies—the head, neck, feet, tail and feathers—that make each bird look different. Start out by drawing the biggest, simplest shape—the body—first.

Sizing up

Before you start drawing the body parts, look at the size of the bird's head, feet, tail and so on in relation to its body. For example, the owl's head is large compared to its body, but the ostrich has a very tiny head. Compare the lengths of body parts, too. Notice how long the ostrich's neck is, while the owl doesn't seem to have any neck at all.

Each bird beak has its own size and shape. Compare the size of the beak to the rest of the head. Notice that the macaw's beak is as wide as its head. On the other hand, this blue tit's beak is only as big as its eye. Where does the beak join the oval of the head? Is it pointing straight out or down? Check these details before adding the beak to your drawing.

Lining up

Here's a helpful hint to line up, or position, different parts of a bird's body in your sketch. Hold your pencil upright at arm's length in front of the bird. Close one eye and look up and down the pencil. Note the location of each body part with respect to this imaginary line formed by your pencil. The robin drawn here has its head and feet stretched over to the left of the pencil, while its wings and tail fall to the right. Try holding your pencil out horizontally, too. Note how this bird's head lines up with its outstretched wing.

Finishing up

Bring your bird to life by adding some details. Notice the direction from which the light is coming and shade in the shadows. Finally, add tones for the dark patches and special markings of your bird.

Nature in Winter

When it comes to surviving the snow and cold, you'll be surprised to find out how much people and birds are alike. Make a simple birdfeeder this winter to attract birds to your yard for a closer look. Find out where to look for active winter insects, as well as those that hibernate. Even spring flowers aren't too far away — just dig away some snow to get a glimpse of the new season's promise. This winter, add nature watching to your list of outdoor activities.

Watching winter insects

Have you ever gone camping in the summer? Did you go to sleep listening to the whine of mosquitoes in the tent and wake up scratching in the morning? If the bugs bugged you, try camping in the winter. It may be chilly but at least most of the bugs will be gone. Or will they?

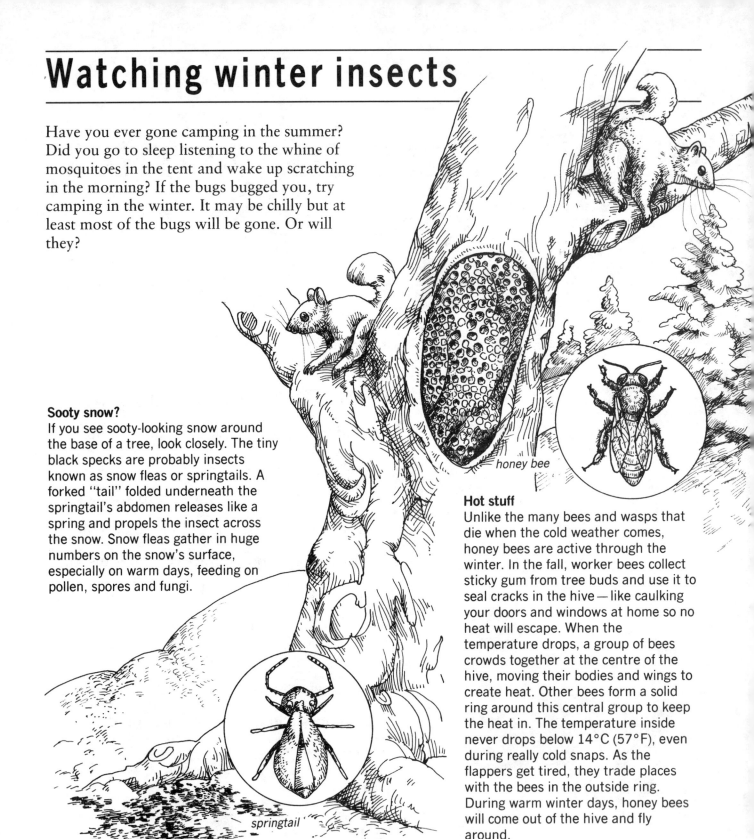

honey bee

springtail

Sooty snow?

If you see sooty-looking snow around the base of a tree, look closely. The tiny black specks are probably insects known as snow fleas or springtails. A forked "tail" folded underneath the springtail's abdomen releases like a spring and propels the insect across the snow. Snow fleas gather in huge numbers on the snow's surface, especially on warm days, feeding on pollen, spores and fungi.

Hot stuff

Unlike the many bees and wasps that die when the cold weather comes, honey bees are active through the winter. In the fall, worker bees collect sticky gum from tree buds and use it to seal cracks in the hive — like caulking your doors and windows at home so no heat will escape. When the temperature drops, a group of bees crowds together at the centre of the hive, moving their bodies and wings to create heat. Other bees form a solid ring around this central group to keep the heat in. The temperature inside never drops below 14°C (57°F), even during really cold snaps. As the flappers get tired, they trade places with the bees in the outside ring. During warm winter days, honey bees will come out of the hive and fly around.

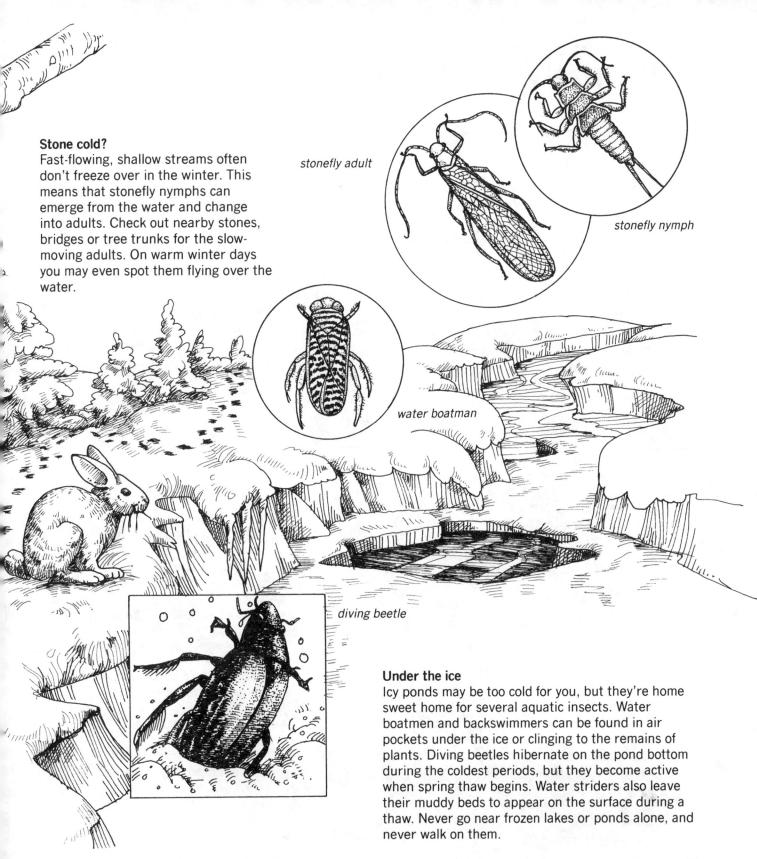

Stone cold?

Fast-flowing, shallow streams often don't freeze over in the winter. This means that stonefly nymphs can emerge from the water and change into adults. Check out nearby stones, bridges or tree trunks for the slow-moving adults. On warm winter days you may even spot them flying over the water.

stonefly adult

stonefly nymph

water boatman

diving beetle

Under the ice

Icy ponds may be too cold for you, but they're home sweet home for several aquatic insects. Water boatmen and backswimmers can be found in air pockets under the ice or clinging to the remains of plants. Diving beetles hibernate on the pond bottom during the coldest periods, but they become active when spring thaw begins. Water striders also leave their muddy beds to appear on the surface during a thaw. Never go near frozen lakes or ponds alone, and never walk on them.

Winter disguises

Some insects spend the winter as eggs, others as larvae, pupae or even adults. Each stage has its own advantages for winter survival.

Eggs are surprisingly good at resisting the cold. Some mosquito eggs are even adapted to hatch in the water left by melting snow.

Larvae that are well hidden and surrounded by food, such as the grubs inside galls, can eat and grow through the winter.

Pupae, such as the cocoons of moths, don't feed at all during winter but spend the time waiting to turn into an adult in spring. The sealed cocoon helps protect the insect inside from bad weather and hungry predators.

Mourning cloak butterflies and some other insects hibernate as adults, allowing them to mate and start a family very early in spring.

Where to look

You can find insects hibernating just about anywhere in winter. Some spend winter underground; others hide under stones, rocks, rotting logs, bark, leaves and man-made structures such as porches, siding and shingles. A few sneaky insects try to move inside your home for a nice warm winter.

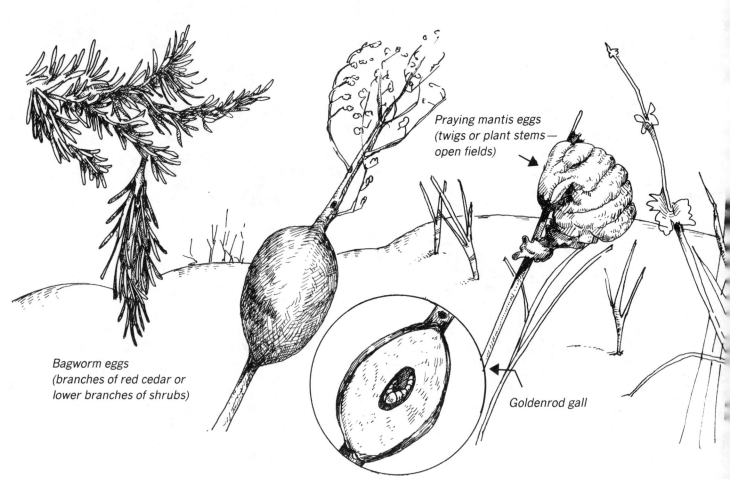

Bagworm eggs
(branches of red cedar or
lower branches of shrubs)

Praying mantis eggs
(twigs or plant stems—
open fields)

Goldenrod gall

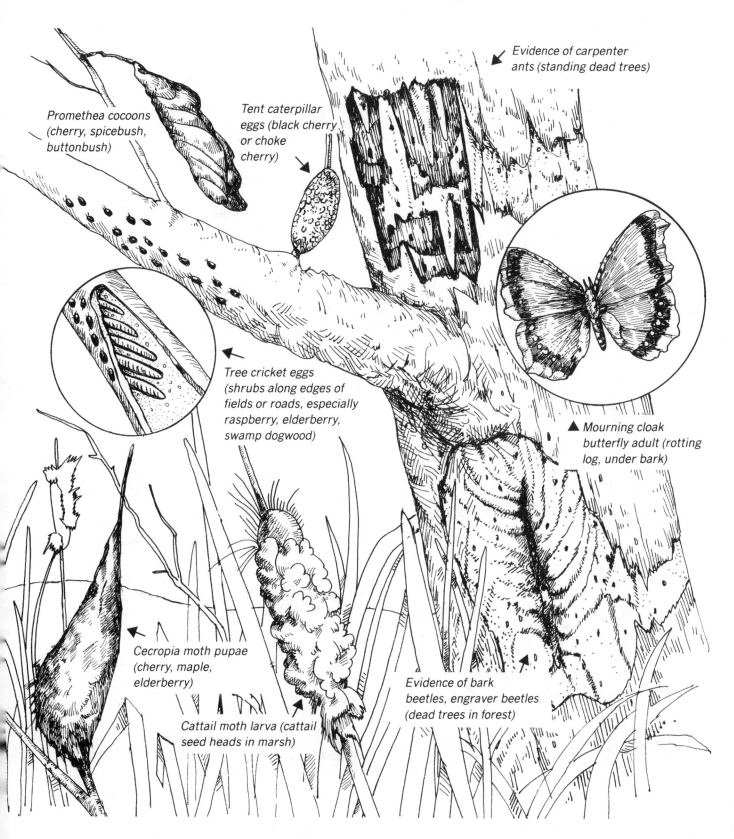

Promethea cocoons (cherry, spicebush, buttonbush)

Tent caterpillar eggs (black cherry or choke cherry)

Evidence of carpenter ants (standing dead trees)

Tree cricket eggs (shrubs along edges of fields or roads, especially raspberry, elderberry, swamp dogwood)

Mourning cloak butterfly adult (rotting log, under bark)

Cecropia moth pupae (cherry, maple, elderberry)

Cattail moth larva (cattail seed heads in marsh)

Evidence of bark beetles, engraver beetles (dead trees in forest)

Busy bees (and wasps)

You may not want a bee in your bonnet, but a bee's nest in your neighbourhood can be fascinating. There are more than 3300 species of bees and wasps in North America, so you're bound to discover some of their amazing nests. Afraid of being told to buzz off by a busy bee? Just wait until winter when most nest owners have been killed by the cold. Even if the nest is active, with bees or wasps moving in and out, you can keep a safe distance and still identify the owners by the shape of their nest. Here's a mini-guide to some of the most common nests. Try to match the nests to the owners below. (Answers on page 158.)

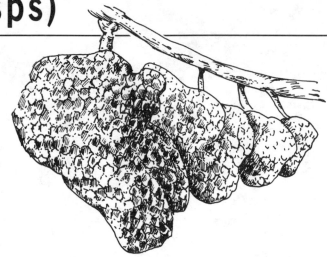

Wax works

Hundreds of other workers and I spend our days making six-sided cells out of beeswax and gluing thousands of cells together to make honeycombs. You can find our nests in holes, hollow trees or rock crevices, but you may also see our honeycombs hanging in the open from a tree branch. What am I?

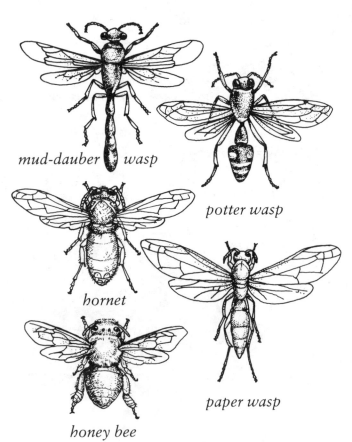

mud-dauber wasp

potter wasp

hornet

paper wasp

honey bee

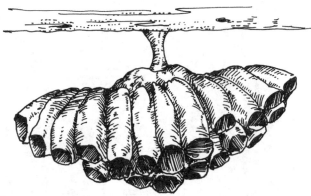

Paper nests

I've been making pulp and paper much longer than people. By chewing up the stringy fibres of rotting wood or plant stems and mixing it with saliva, I produce a pulp-like material. This is shaped into a single layer of open-ended cells that looks like papier-mâché when dry. My nest hangs by a short stalk beneath eaves, porches and other overhangs. What am I?

Pottery nests

I shape my tiny pot-like nest out of little balls of clay or mud and then attach the nest to a twig. After one egg is laid in the pot, I seal it up and fly away. What am I?

Wrapping paper

My paper nest hangs from trees, shrubs or the eaves of buildings. As the queen, I started the nest as one cell, but it got bigger and bigger as more workers were born to help me. The outside of my nest is wrapped up in sheets of paper, like a Christmas present. The only door is a small hole at the bottom or side. What am I?

Organ pipes

In sheltered spots like eaves, sheds or bridges, you'll find my long, tubular nests made from balls of mud. People think my nests look like organ pipes. What am I?

Breakfast in bed

Instead of flying back and forth to feed their hungry babies, some wasp mothers are really organized. A female potter wasp hunts down caterpillars, stings them and then stuffs the paralyzed insects into her tiny, pot-shaped nest before laying an egg inside. When her larva hatches, it has all the food it needs, without having to get out of bed.

Winter wonders

Did you know that some plants hibernate in the winter, just as some animals do? When you get the winter blues and you're longing for a breath of spring, you can get a sneak preview of the spring to come by searching for April's flowers below the snow.

You'll need:
a trowel
a field guide to wildflowers
a pencil
paper

1. Visit a wood lot where you've seen spring flowers blooming in past years. If you can remember just where certain flowers bloomed, that'll make it easier. If not, look for open spaces away from tree trunks.
2. If the snow is deep, use your trowel to clear a patch of forest floor. With your hands, gently brush away the fallen leaves and look for the leaves of over-wintering wildflowers. These are flowers whose stems have died back to the ground, but whose roots and, sometimes, basal leaves are still alive. Instead of starting out from seed in the spring, the plant will grow from its hibernating roots. Some flowers may appear as a ring of green leaves hugging the ground, while others may show the remains of last year's dead leaves through which the new season's growth will appear.
3. Look for wild ginger, hepatica, bloodroot and others. You may need your field guide to identify the plants.
4. Cover the "sleeping" flowers back up with the leaves and snow to keep them protected from the cold.
5. Make a note of where you found flowers by sketching a small map. Return in the spring to see what has bloomed. If you record the locations of spring wildflowers in bloom, you can find them much more easily next winter.

Nature's antifreeze

If trees are 80 to 90% water, do they freeze solid in cold winters? The answer is yes, but it doesn't hurt the trees. As the cold weather approaches, the concentration of sugar in the tree's cells increases, acting as a sort of antifreeze. However, the sugar concentration is not enough to stop the trees from freezing solid during the coldest parts of winter. In the early spring, when the nights are freezing and days are milder, the higher sugar concentration in the sap causes the sap to thaw by day, although it may still freeze at night. It is this alternate freezing and thawing within the tree that forces the sap to flow. Try this simple activity to see how sugar helps lower the freezing temperature of water.

You'll need:
2 plastic cups
water
sugar
a spoon
a freezer

1. Fill each cup half full of water.
2. To one cup, add 2 heaping spoonfuls of sugar. Stir until the sugar is dissolved.

3. Place both cups in a freezer. After an hour, compare the contents of each container. You should find that the sugar-water mixture has not frozen solid, while the cup of pure water contains solid ice. Eventually, the sugar-water will freeze too because of the very cold temperature of your freezer.

How does it work?
The sugar in the water acts as an antifreeze, lowering the freezing point of the water. Therefore, the pure water will freeze solid more quickly and at a higher temperature than the sugar-water. If you could set your freezer temperature to 0°C (32°F) (the freezing point of water), you would find that the pure water would be frozen, while the sugar-water would not be frozen solid.

On the move

How do birds find their way from summer breeding grounds to winter feeding areas? Why do they migrate? Unfortunately, birds can't talk, so we can't know for certain their answers to these questions. But we can ask an ornithologist (a scientist who studies birds). Here Dr. Ian Kirkham answers some of the most often asked questions about migration.

Q. What is migration?

A. Migration is the seasonal movement of birds and other animals. There are three types of migration: diurnal, nocturnal and altitudinal. Diurnal migration takes place during the day (diurnal means day). Birds that fly at night are called nocturnal migrants (nocturnal means night). Unlike diurnal and nocturnal migration, altitudinal migration may take only a few minutes. In the fall, birds nesting high up in the mountains fly down to lower slopes or valleys where winter conditions are better. In the spring, the birds return to the higher altitudes. Instead of flying thousands of kilometres to reach a suitable habitat, altitudinal migrants can get there much faster and easier—a bit like taking an elevator!

Q. Why do birds migrate?

A. There may be several reasons for migration. It may be triggered by reduced hours of sunlight or by a shortage of food. Or maybe cold temperatures start birds migrating or, in the spring, the instinct to return to breeding grounds. But not all birds pay attention to these signs, since not all species migrate.

Q. How do birds find their way?

A. Some birds, such as young geese, follow their parents during migration, but the young of many other species have to find their own way south. How they do it has puzzled scientists for a long time. Some birds may follow mountain ranges and coastlines, like a map. Others, however, migrate across oceans where no landmarks are found. One theory is that migrating birds use the stars or angle of the sun to help find their way, like pilots and sailors do. Although there are still some mysteries about migration, one thing is certain; birds not only get where they're going, but also get there at almost the same time every year.

Q. How far do birds travel when they migrate?

A. It depends on the bird. Lots of North American birds travel to Central or South America and back, a distance of as much as 3000 kilometres (1800 miles). But some amazing migrants travel even farther. The Arctic Tern, for example, flies from the far North to the southern tip of South America and the edge of Antarctica's pack ice. Its round-trip migration is farther than the distance around the earth, making it the longest migration of any animal.

Migration marvels

□ *Whooping Cranes fly from southern Texas to northern Alberta every year to nest in Wood Buffalo National Park. Because the cranes always return to the same place, scientists can count exactly how many there are from year to year.*

□ *In San Juan Capistrano, California, people almost set their watches by the massive return of the swallows. It happens every year on March 19.*

□ *In Pembroke, Ontario, an annual Festival of Swallows is celebrated in August. Nearly 200 000 swallows invade the town on a migration stopover.*

Believe it or not

In ancient times, people had strange ideas about the seasonal appearance and disappearance of some birds.

□ *Aristotle, the ancient Greek philosopher, believed that birds didn't go anywhere, but simply changed their identity with another species. For instance, he said that as summer approached, the European Robin became a European Redstart. This explained why the redstart appeared and the robin disappeared.*

□ *Some naturalists thought that only large birds could migrate across oceans. They believed that smaller birds hitchhiked on the backs of others.*

□ *In 1703, an Englishman wrote that birds flew to the moon over a period of 60 days and then went into hibernation.*

Warming up in winter

If you live in a climate where the winters are cold and snowy, you know that trying to keep warm is a major pastime. Like people, birds have also developed different ways to keep from freezing. In fact, we have learned some of our winter survival tricks from birds!

Feeling down

Many people wear down jackets or vests in the winter for warmth. Down feathers — the soft feathers found on many newly hatched birds and the undercoats of ducks and geese — are great for warmth. Air is trapped between the feathers, acting as an insulator to keep your body heat in and cold air out. Birds also fluff up their natural covering of feathers to trap air and keep warm. Some species can puff up to almost three times their normal size.

Bundle up!

When the winter winds blow, it's time to pull on an extra sweater — and maybe even long underwear. Birds don't have clothes but they *do* grow more feathers for winter warmth. The American Goldfinch, for example, has about a thousand more feathers in winter than in summer.

Snuggle up

Huddling together is a great way of fighting the cold. Chickadees gather in small groups in tree holes to pool body heat. As many as a million starlings may roost together on rooftops, building ledges, in evergreens or other sheltered areas. Why these gigantic slumber parties? Some experts believe that the combined body heat and mass of the birds helps them stay warm and reduces the effect of wind chill.

A nice cold bed

You've heard of the expression "blanket of snow." Well, the Ruffed Grouse takes it seriously. On cold nights, it may dive into a bank or drift of deep, fluffy snow to sleep. The air spaces in the snow provide excellent insulation and the snow itself acts as a perfect camouflage. Smaller birds, such as American Tree Sparrows, Common Redpolls and Snow Buntings, also take shelter under snow in very cold weather. If you think a bed of snow is for the birds, think again. The Inuit in the far North sleep in snow homes, and people stranded because of plane crashes often survive by curling up in a snow bed.

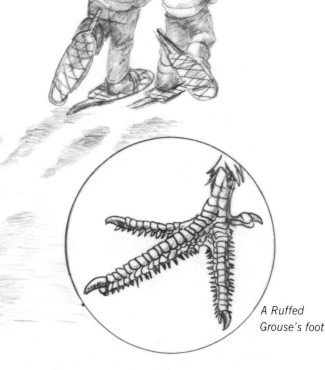

A Ruffed Grouse's foot

Feathered snowshoes

To get around in deep snow, some people wear snowshoes. The snowshoe spreads your weight over a larger surface area and allows you to walk on top of the snow, rather than through it. Some birds grow their own miniature snowshoes in winter. Scaly growths along the toes of Ruffed Grouse help the birds travel easily over the powdery woodland snow. Similarly, ptarmigans grow extra feathers between their toes to help them walk on top of the snow.

Feed the birds

How can you get birds to visit your yard? Invite them for a meal! Feeding birds is not only fun; it's a great way to see birds up close and find out about their behaviour.

In areas where the winters are cold, many birds become dependent on feeders to help them get through the season. The energy they get from food helps keep them warm. Food supply, not temperature, is often the key to winter survival. Because of this, it is important to keep feeding your feathered friends once you start. Feed them all through the winter and into the spring, until nature can once again take over with its own supply of seeds, berries and insects.

Although you can go to a store and buy a ready-made birdfeeder, you can also make a terrific feeder out of a few easy-to-find materials. Try some of these ideas for attracting and feeding birds. Make several feeders and hang them around your garden or school yard.

Coconut feeder

You may think coconuts are for monkeys, but this one is for the birds!

You'll need: one coconut
a hand drill
a small saw
1-1.5 m (3-5 feet) of thin, bendable wire

1. Drill a hole in the coconut and drain out the milk.
2. Cut a quarter off one end of the coconut, using the saw. Ask an adult to help you do this so you don't cut yourself.

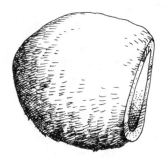

3. Drill two holes near the cut edge, one on either side. Thread the wire through the holes so that the coconut can be hung from a branch or other support as shown.

4. Some birds will eat the coconut meat, but you can also fill the cavity with seed as an added treat.

Things to watch for

Watch the birds that flock to your homemade feeder. You can discover a lot about them just by being a keen observer. Here are a few things to watch for:

□ What kinds of food do different birds prefer? Birds, like people, have likes and dislikes when it comes to eating. You may find that woodpeckers, nuthatches and other insect-eaters are attracted by suet, while seed-eaters, such as Blue Jays and Evening Grosbeaks, prefer sunflower seeds.

□ Where do the birds like to eat? Some birds, such as Blue Jays and cardinals, are happy feeding as high as 1.5 m (1.5 yards) or more above ground. Juncos, on the other hand, often eat on the ground, eating the seed spilled from feeders above.

□ Which birds spend the longest time feeding? Different birds have very different eating habits. Chickadees, for instance, rush in for a quick nibble and rush away again, only to return within a minute or two to repeat the performance. On the other hand a Mourning Dove may gracefully glide in for a landing and settle down to eat at its leisure.

□ Are some birds more aggressive than others? After you watch your feeder for a while, the "personalities" of birds begin to show. In general, small birds are scared off by larger and noisier ones. Aggressive species, such as starlings and Blue Jays, stand out in a crowd.

□ What time of day is most popular for feeding? You may get a flurry of activity at your feeder at certain times of day. Once you have figured out the local feeding schedule, you can choose the best times for feeder watching.

Suet log feeder

Make a woodpecker's life easier with this simple-to-make feeder.

You'll need: a small log (about as long as your arm and a bit thicker) of poplar or birch
a hand drill
an eye-screw
30 cm (1 foot) of strong, bendable wire
suet

1. Make suet by melting beef fat (not pork because it's too salty) and then cooling it.
2. Drill several holes 1-2 cm (½ to ¾ of an inch) deep and 2.5 cm (1 inch) wide around your log. To get holes this big, use the largest drill bit and then enlarge the hole around the edges.
3. Attach an eye-screw to one end.
4. Fill the holes with suet.
5. Hang the log with wire from a branch.

Tin can feeder

What do you get when you cross a juice can with two pie plates? A nifty birdfeeder of course!

You'll need: a clean tin can, such as a large juice can, with both ends removed
tin snips
2 foil pie plates
scissors
75 cm (2.5 feet) of strong, bendable wire
birdseed
60 cm (2 feet) of string

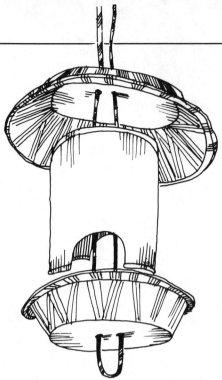

1. Ask an adult to cut two semi-circles on opposite sides of the bottom edge of your tin can with tin snips.

2. In each of your pie plates, make two small holes about 4 cm (1.5 inches) apart, near the middle.

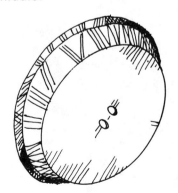

3. Assemble your materials as shown. Thread the wire through the pie plates and can so that the two loose ends are at the top.

4. Twist the ends of the wire together about 10 cm (4 inches) above the top pie plate.

5. Slide the top pie plate up the wire so that you can fill the can with seed. As the birds eat from the bottom tray, the seed will come through the semi-circles and refill the tray.

6. This feeder can be hung from a branch with string or placed on a table or other sturdy platform. Squirrels may help themselves at a table, though.

7. To refill the can, simply slide the top pie plate up the wires and pour in the seed.

Onion bag feeder

You can feed the birds and recycle at the same time. Use the net bag that onions come in to make this odour-free feeder.

You'll need: suet
  net bag, like the ones onions are sold in (do not use wire mesh)
  30 cm (1 foot) of string
  birdseed

1. Make suet by melting beef fat (not pork because it's too salty) and then cooling it.
2. Shape the suet into a ball the size of a tennis ball and roll it in birdseed.
3. Place the ball in the net bag and hang it from a branch with string.

Pine cone feeder

Give nuthatches, chickadees and other insect-eaters a suet-stuffed treat.

You'll need: suet
  peanut butter (optional)
  pine cones (the short, squat cones of red pine work well)
  an eye-screw
  30 cm (1 foot) of string or thin, bendable wire

1. Make your suet by melting beef fat (not pork because it is too salty) and then cooling it.
2. Roll your pine cone in the suet or a mixture of suet and peanut butter so that the nooks and crannies are filled.

3. Insert an eye-screw in the cone as shown.
4. Attach a string or wire to the eye-screw and hang your feeder from a branch.

Peanut feeder

Here's a nutty idea for attracting birds to your garden or school yard. You may even get some squirrels, too.

You'll need: raw peanuts in the shell
  string or yarn

1. Tie the peanuts in a row with your string or yarn.
2. Hang the string from a branch.

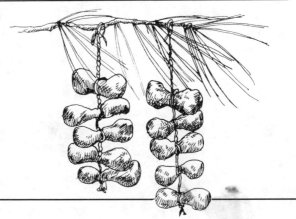

Nature up Close

Think all bugs look alike? Discover the differences between butterflies and moths, and find out why spiders and other bug-like creatures aren't true insects. Learn to identify insect-eating birds simply by looking at the shape of their beaks. Then head to the trees for a woodpecker hole hunt or an evening owl prowl. While you're in the woods, collect a few cones and bring them home for some simple experiments. Even the flowers in your home or garden can tell fascinating stories if you take a closer look. Get nose to nose with nature and you'll be amazed at what you see.

Who's an insect and who isn't?

Do all of the creatures on this page look like insects to you? Well, they're not. Some of them are insect impostors. How can you tell real insects from non-insects?

All adult insects share certain characteristics. (Immature insects are so different that there's no easy way to tell them—only practice.) All adult insects have:

☐ 6 legs
☐ 3 body parts: head, thorax, abdomen
☐ 2 antennae
☐ most have 1 or 2 pairs of wings

Now try guessing who's an insect and who's not. (Answers on page 158.)

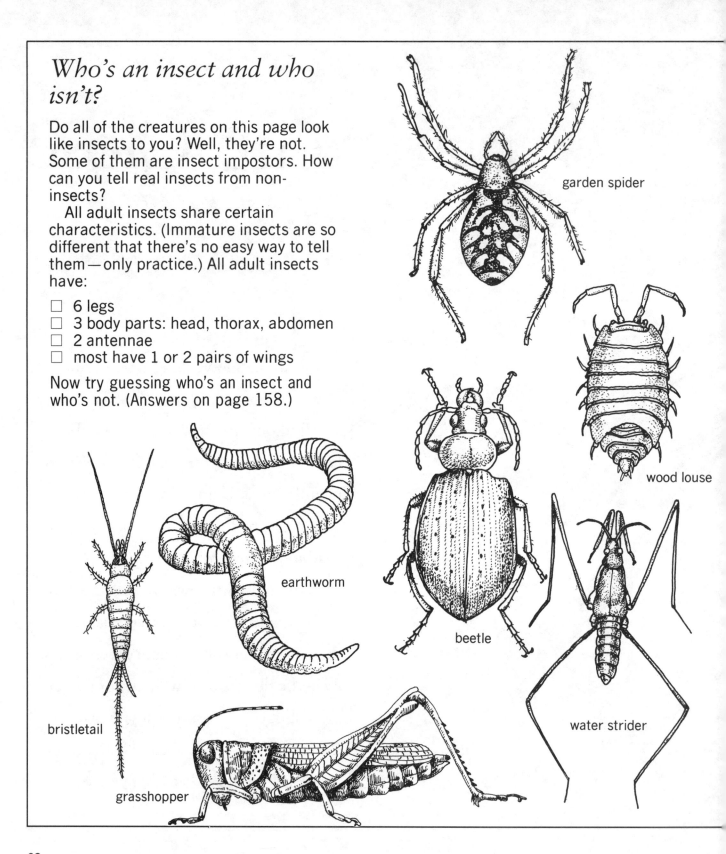

garden spider

wood louse

earthworm

beetle

water strider

bristletail

grasshopper

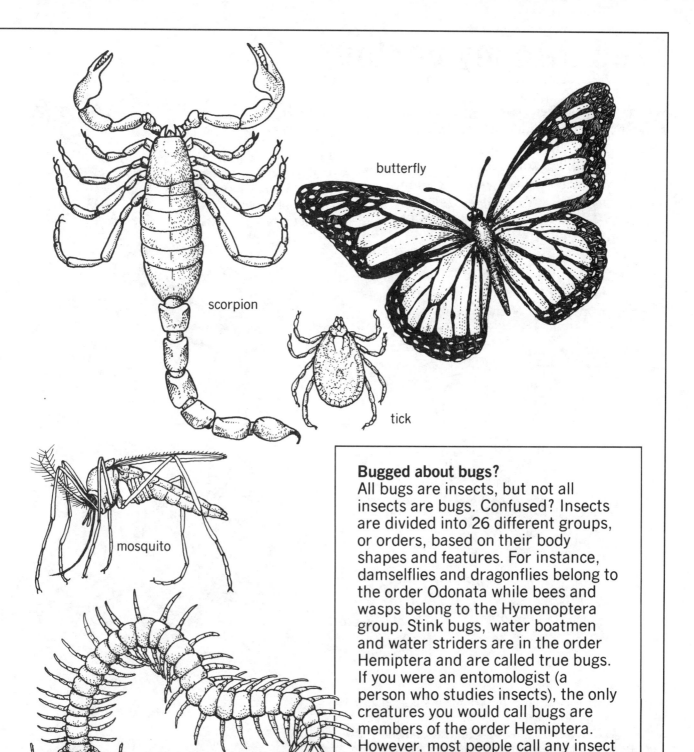

scorpion

butterfly

tick

mosquito

centipede

Bugged about bugs?
All bugs are insects, but not all insects are bugs. Confused? Insects are divided into 26 different groups, or orders, based on their body shapes and features. For instance, damselflies and dragonflies belong to the order Odonata while bees and wasps belong to the Hymenoptera group. Stink bugs, water boatmen and water striders are in the order Hemiptera and are called true bugs. If you were an entomologist (a person who studies insects), the only creatures you would call bugs are members of the order Hemiptera. However, most people call any insect a bug. And lots of people even call non-insects (like spiders) bugs.

Step into my parlour . . .

When you go spider watching, you can see different kinds of spiders as well as the different traps they use to catch their prey. Spiders spin all kinds of different webs including cobwebs, sheet webs and funnel webs. Wanderers have some neat homes too. Take a look at some of these traps and how they're used to catch supper.

Cobweb

When you forget to dust in the corners of your bedroom, you might find that a spider has moved in. Cobwebs are common in houses. Spiders use them to trap house flies. ▷

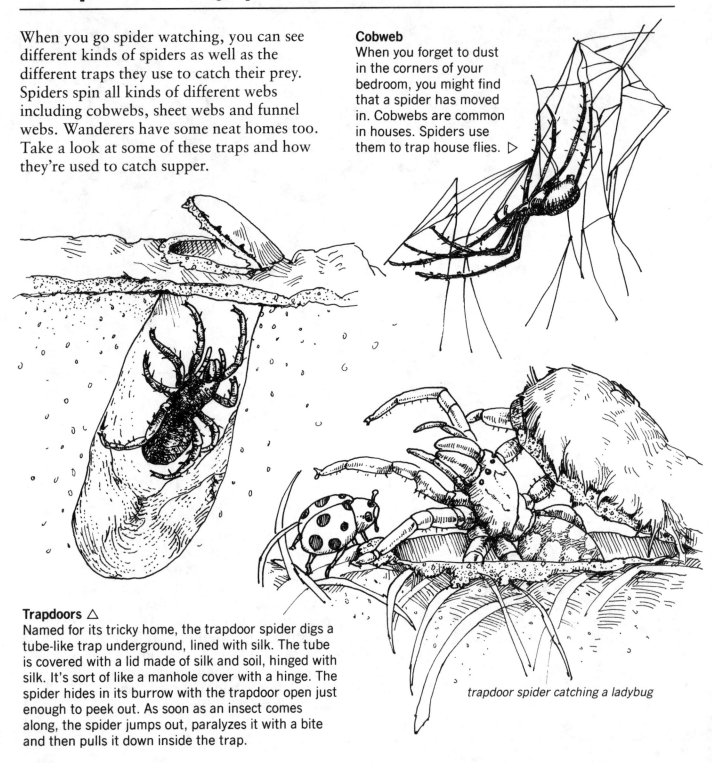

trapdoor spider catching a ladybug

Trapdoors △

Named for its tricky home, the trapdoor spider digs a tube-like trap underground, lined with silk. The tube is covered with a lid made of silk and soil, hinged with silk. It's sort of like a manhole cover with a hinge. The spider hides in its burrow with the trapdoor open just enough to peek out. As soon as an insect comes along, the spider jumps out, paralyzes it with a bite and then pulls it down inside the trap.

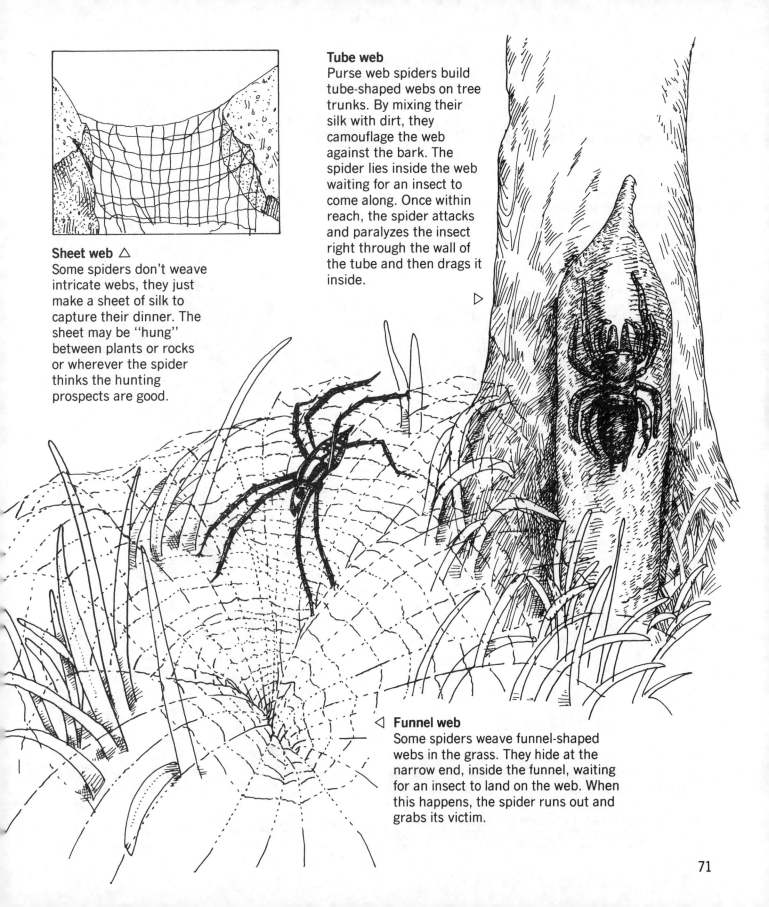

Sheet web △
Some spiders don't weave intricate webs, they just make a sheet of silk to capture their dinner. The sheet may be "hung" between plants or rocks or wherever the spider thinks the hunting prospects are good.

Tube web
Purse web spiders build tube-shaped webs on tree trunks. By mixing their silk with dirt, they camouflage the web against the bark. The spider lies inside the web waiting for an insect to come along. Once within reach, the spider attacks and paralyzes the insect right through the wall of the tube and then drags it inside.

▷

◁ **Funnel web**
Some spiders weave funnel-shaped webs in the grass. They hide at the narrow end, inside the funnel, waiting for an insect to land on the web. When this happens, the spider runs out and grabs its victim.

Web watching . . .

Why not invite a spider to spin for you, and see how it's really done?

You'll need:
a forked branch
a large glass container, like a 4-L
 (4-quart) mustard jar
a piece of fine screening
an elastic band
insects
a plant mister with water

1. Place the branch in the container.
2. Collect an orb-weaver spider, such as a common garden spider, from the wild and gently place it on the branch.
3. Cover the container with the screen and secure it with the elastic.

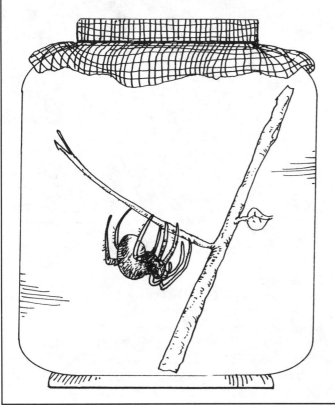

4. Watch as the spider spins its web. Once the web is built, add a couple of live flying insects, such as flies or mosquitoes, and watch the action.

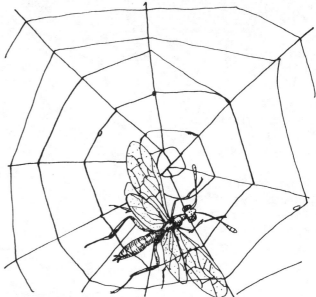

5. Spray the web with a fine mist of water to provide your spider with some moisture.

6. Let your spider go after a day or so.

. . . and collecting

Unlike birds' nests, spider webs can be collected with no danger to their owners. Spiders rebuild their webs frequently and quickly. You can collect different shapes or patterns of webs, or do crafts using spider webs.

You'll need:
a can of clear spray lacquer
a piece of heavy black paper
scissors
clear plastic wrap

1. Locate a good spider web.
2. Make sure the spider is gone, then spray the web lightly with lacquer three or four times until it is stiff.

3. Place a piece of heavy paper right under the web.
4. Very carefully cut the strands that attach the web to its supports.

5. Have your paper ready to catch the web as it comes loose.

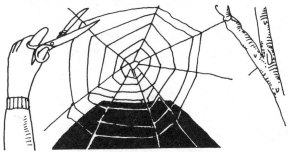

6. Spray another light coating of lacquer on to the paper to make the web stick.

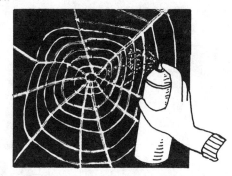

7. Cover your web and paper with clear plastic wrap if you want to keep it for a collection.
8. You can also use different colours of spray paint to make colourful spider web pictures.

How to tell a butterfly from a moth

Butterflies and moths are closely related, like first cousins. Many people have trouble telling them apart, but once you know what to look for, it's easy to tell which is which.

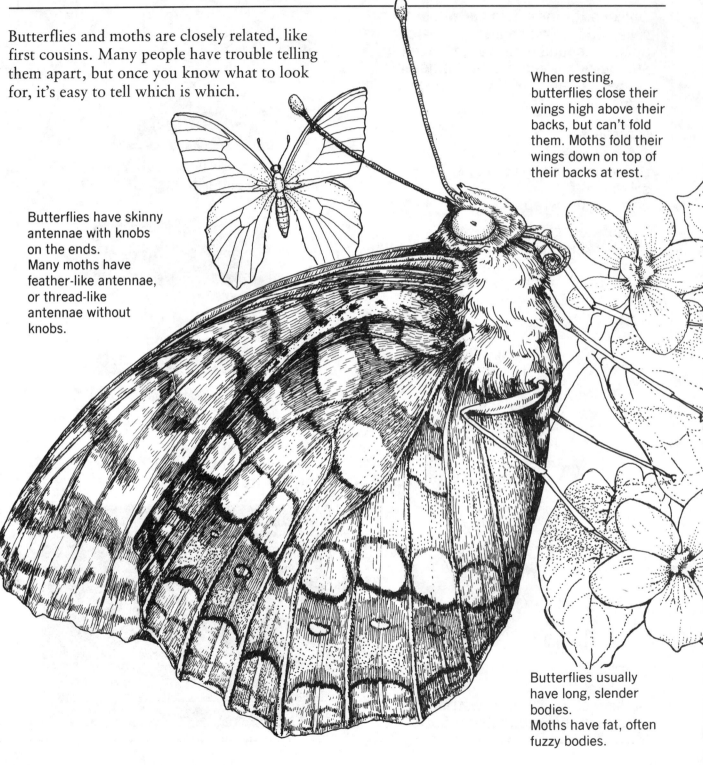

Butterflies have skinny antennae with knobs on the ends.
Many moths have feather-like antennae, or thread-like antennae without knobs.

When resting, butterflies close their wings high above their backs, but can't fold them. Moths fold their wings down on top of their backs at rest.

Butterflies usually have long, slender bodies.
Moths have fat, often fuzzy bodies.

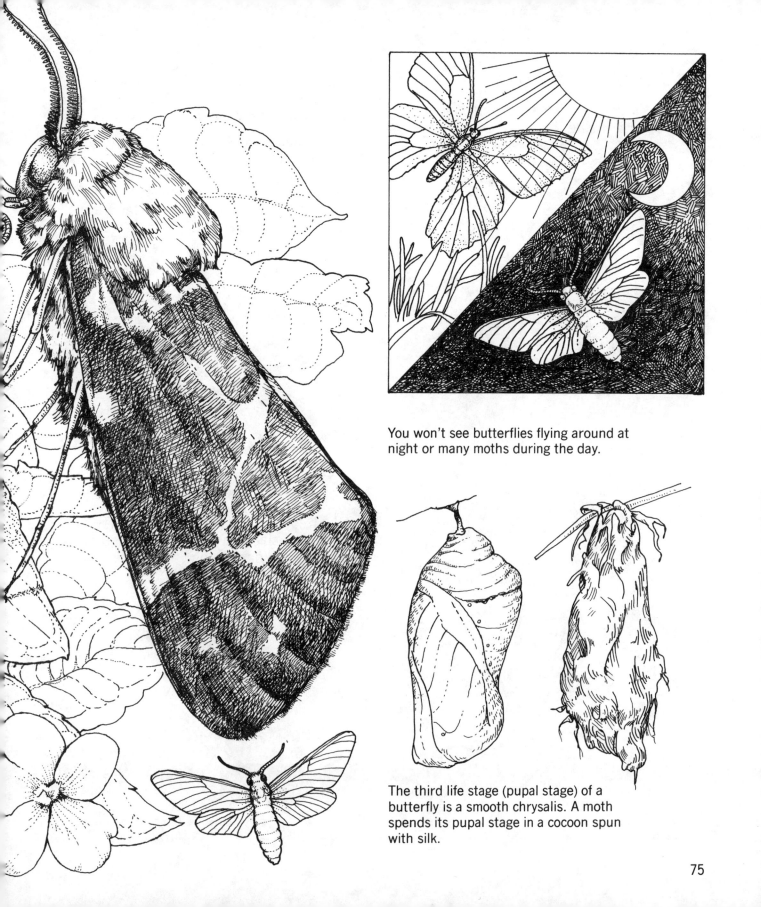

You won't see butterflies flying around at night or many moths during the day.

The third life stage (pupal stage) of a butterfly is a smooth chrysalis. A moth spends its pupal stage in a cocoon spun with silk.

Dissecting a flower

Try dissecting a flower to get a look at the parts inside.

wild geranium

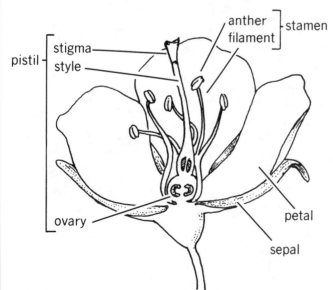

You'll need:

a single, regular flower in full bloom (tulip, Easter lily, tiger lily for example)

1. You'll see six petal-like parts. The three outside parts are the sepals. (On some flowers these will look like green leaves.) The sepals protect the flower when it is in the bud stage. Gently pull the sepals off.

sepal

2. Next, look at the petals. Their colour, shape or size is probably designed to attract pollinators, but the petals also protect the sex organs of the flower from drying out.

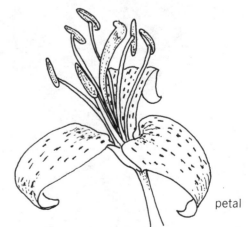

petal

3. Take off the petals and look for the stamens — the flower's male organs. They look like thin stalks, called filaments, with club-like heads. The heads are called anthers and are usually yellow, but may be other colours, including black in the tulip. Gently touch an anther with your finger. If it is ripe, a yellow (usually) dust-like substance, called pollen, will rub off onto your finger. Try to see where the base of the stamen is attached.

stamen

4. Pick off the stamens, leaving the central pistil, or female organ. The pistil has three parts: a swollen base, called the ovary, where the seeds form; a stalk-like style; and an enlarged head, called a stigma, where the pollen must land in order to fertilize the flower. Try to find all these parts.

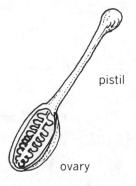

pistil

ovary

5. Different flowers will vary in their structure. Some have many separate pistils, for example, while others may have no styles. The basic parts, however, should still be visible. When you're admiring the flowers in your house, garden or neighbourhood park, take a moment to see if you can find the different parts in various flowers.

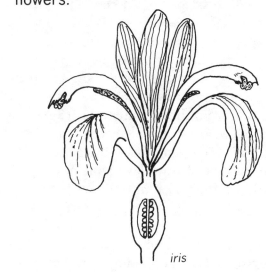

iris

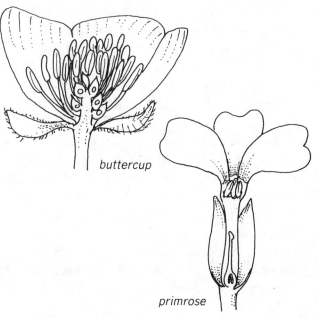

buttercup

primrose

Mini food factory

Plants don't have to go out and hunt for food; they make their own food. The leaves of most plants act like mini food factories where they make food called carbohydrates, or sugars, for the rest of the plant. To make this food, leaves need three essential ingredients: water from the soil; carbon dioxide from the air; and energy from sunlight. This process of making food for the plant is called photosynthesis.

During photosynthesis, water is drawn into the plant through the roots and travels up the stem to the leaves. The carbon dioxide from the air enters the leaves through tiny pores called stomata. The stomata can open or close, depending on the amount of water available in the plant, so that if there is a lot of water present, the stomata open, allowing some water to escape while letting the carbon dioxide enter. With the final ingredient of sunlight, the process of making food can begin.

The chlorophyll, or green colouring, in leaves uses the sun's energy to start the chemical reaction that eventually produces carbohydrates and oxygen. The carbohydrates produced are carried to other parts of the plant in the liquid sap that flows through special tubes in the stem. The stored food is used to help the plant grow. The oxygen that is produced in the chemical reaction is released into the air through the stomata. Since water is not only an ingredient in photosynthesis, but also moves out of the leaves when the stomata are open during photosynthesis, a lot of water is necessary for the food factory to function.

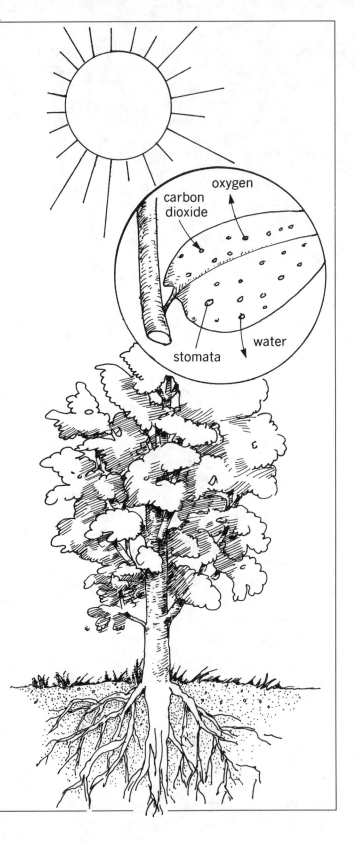

Sweaty trees?

When you're hot, your body sweats in order to help cool you down. Trees also sweat, but not to cool off. It's their way of getting rid of too much water. Except in very dry periods, leaves continually lose water through tiny holes called stomata. This loss of water is called transpiration. As water is lost from the leaves, it creates a sort of vacuum in the xylem. This draws more water up from the roots below. Although the plants absorb some of the water they draw up, most of the water is released back into the air. With some simple materials, you can see transpiration in action by capturing some of the water lost from a plant indoors or outdoors.

You'll need:
a plastic bag
a plant (not one with thick or waxy leaves)
string
water

1. In the morning (sunny days are best), put a plastic bag over a healthy leaf and tie the bag tightly shut with string. Be sure not to damage the leaf stem. If you're using a houseplant, make sure it is well watered.
2. Check your bag at the end of the day. You should see water droplets inside, caused by the plant's transpiration.

Drink up

When you take up a drink through a straw, your sucking action pulls the liquid up the straw and causes more liquid to flow into the bottom of the straw. Plants also drink through a straw-like system of tubes, called xylem, inside their stems. The thin columns of water rise partly through a phenomenon called capillary action, in which water tends to "stick" together and rise. In addition, the leaves of a plant help to suck up the water by opening their stomata. When water reaches the leaves, most of it escapes through the stomata. The escaping water creates a suction, pulling water up the xylem tubes and causing more water to enter below at the roots. In this way, the column of water remains continuous, like the liquid in your straw. Only when you stop sucking, or you run out of juice, does the straw become empty. In large trees, the water may have to rise more than 30 m (100 feet). Not only does it go a long way, but it also flows very quickly, reaching speeds of 45 m (150 feet) per hour in some trees! To see how water is transported inside a plant, try the Plant Straws activity on the next page.

Plant straws

You can see for yourself how a plant draws water by giving it a drink of a different colour. Here's how.

You'll need:
a sharp knife
a fresh carrot with leaves
3 glasses of water
food colouring (red or blue)
a fresh celery stick with leaves
a white tulip or carnation

1. Cut the tip off the carrot and place the carrot into a glass of water. Add a few drops of food colouring to the water.
2. Place a celery stick in a glass of coloured water.
3. Place a white tulip or carnation in a glass of coloured water.

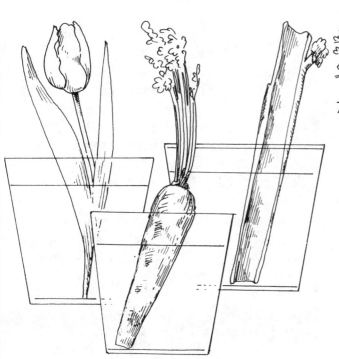

4. Leave all your glasses for several hours.
5. When you return, notice the colouring of the leaves and flowers. You will see that they have taken on some of the colour from the water.

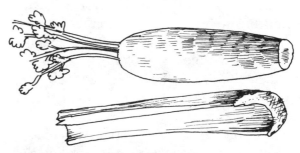

6. Carefully cut the carrot in two lengthwise and look at the core. Remember, the carrot is the root of the plant. The coloured core shows you how the root has drawn water up from the glass and passed it on to the stems and leaves.

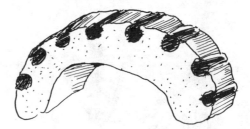

7. Cut a slice from your celery stick. Notice the semi-circle of coloured dots. These are the ends of the xylem tubes that carried the coloured water up the stem of the celery plant. Gently scrape away the outer layer of tissue on the back of the celery stalk so you can see the coloured tubes.

Grass gazing

Why is it that you can mow the lawn every week without hurting the grass, but if you did the same to your flower or vegetable garden, even once, you'd probably finish them off for the season? The answer lies in the way your grass grows. Unlike many plants that grow from their tip, grasses have their actively growing cells farther down the stem at the base of the leaf blades and the nodes (see diagram). So, when you cut the ends of the grass blades off with your mower, you're not affecting the growth zone and it quickly replaces the part cut off. That's when you have to get out the lawn mower again!

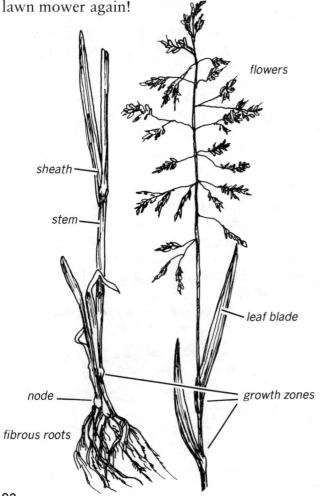

sheath

stem

flowers

leaf blade

node

growth zones

fibrous roots

What good is grass?

Believe it or not, you've probably eaten several varieties of grass already today, especially if you've had any bread, cereal, pasta or rice. All of these foods are made from grass plants. In fact, grasses—mainly corn, wheat, barley, oats, rice, millet and rye—are the most important group of food plants for people in the world. Some form of boiled rice is a basic food for more than half the world's population.

Since we first cultivated grass plants, 10 000 years ago, scientists have continued to improve the basic grass plants for better food production. Even today, wild relatives of these cultivated plants are bred with grass plants to help increase crop resistance to disease, drought and temperature extremes. In addition to feeding people directly, grasses such as sorghum and hay crops make up most of the feed for domesticated animals such as cows and sheep.

Besides providing animals and humans with food, grasses are useful to us in many other ways as well. For instance, bamboo canes are important building materials; reeds are woven into baskets, carpets and furniture (such as wicker); straw is woven into hats; and other grasses are processed to make adhesives, packaging materials and even paper.

Grass up close

You've probably walked on and through millions of blades of grass in your life, but have you ever stopped to take a closer look? Here's your chance. First, head to an unmown ditch or meadow, since the grass will be taller and easier to see and it is more likely to have flowers.

You'll need:
a trowel
a magnifying glass

1. Carefully dig up a small tuft of grass, disturbing the roots as little as possible. Try to find grass that is in flower.

2. Using the illustration on page 82 as a reference, try to find the different parts on your grass, starting with the fibrous roots.

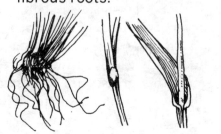

3. Notice how the sheath encloses and protects the stem and then fans out into the leaf blade.

4. Examine the flowers with your magnifying glass. Can you find the pollen-producing anthers and the stigmas? How do you think these flowers are pollinated? Since the flowers are so tiny and not colourful, you can guess that they are not pollinated by insects or birds. When the anthers are ripe with pollen, they hang out from the flower so that the wind can carry the pollen to other plants.

5. When you have finished examining the grass, replant it.

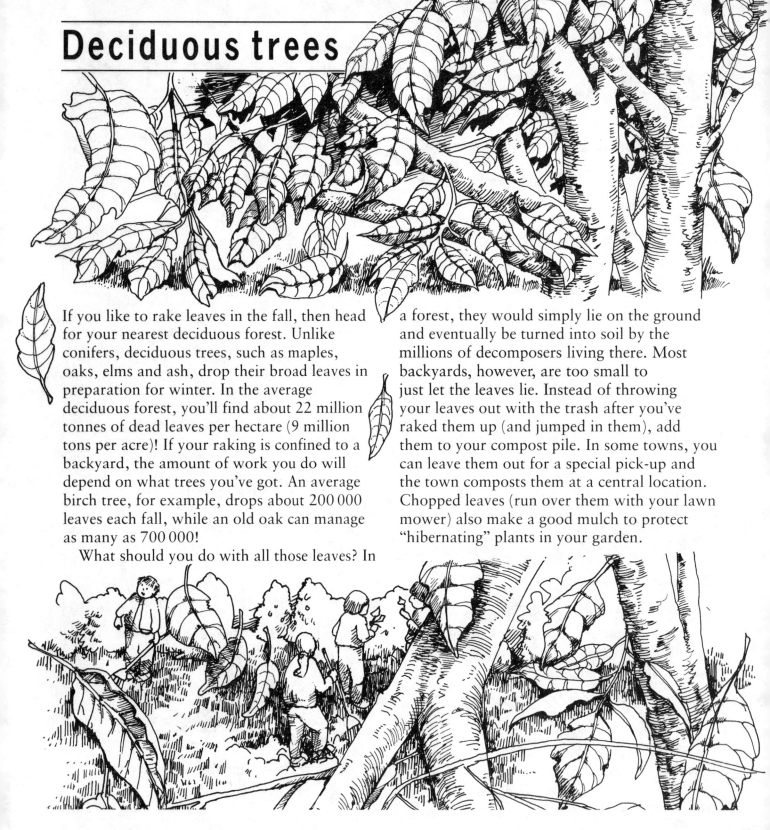

Deciduous trees

If you like to rake leaves in the fall, then head for your nearest deciduous forest. Unlike conifers, deciduous trees, such as maples, oaks, elms and ash, drop their broad leaves in preparation for winter. In the average deciduous forest, you'll find about 22 million tonnes of dead leaves per hectare (9 million tons per acre)! If your raking is confined to a backyard, the amount of work you do will depend on what trees you've got. An average birch tree, for example, drops about 200 000 leaves each fall, while an old oak can manage as many as 700 000!

What should you do with all those leaves? In a forest, they would simply lie on the ground and eventually be turned into soil by the millions of decomposers living there. Most backyards, however, are too small to just let the leaves lie. Instead of throwing your leaves out with the trash after you've raked them up (and jumped in them), add them to your compost pile. In some towns, you can leave them out for a special pick-up and the town composts them at a central location. Chopped leaves (run over them with your lawn mower) also make a good mulch to protect "hibernating" plants in your garden.

Holey leaves

Despite what you may think, deciduous trees don't lose their leaves just to give you a job to do in the fall. The leaves are shed to help stop water loss through their stomata during winter. Since the ground is frozen, the tree cannot drink up any new water, even though it still gives off some water through its trunks and branches during winter. As long as the water loss isn't too severe, the tree will survive until spring.

Although the stomata are too tiny to see at a glance, try this trick to find out where they are.

You'll need:
a stove
water
a pot
a glass jar
some green leaves from a deciduous tree
  (maple, birch, elm, etc.)

1. Boil some water in a pot and pour it into the jar. (Ask an adult to help you.)
2. Dip a leaf into the water.
3. Watch to see what part of the leaf the bubbles are coming from. The heat from the water causes the air inside the leaf to expand and pass out of the leaf through the stomata. If most of your bubbles are coming from the lower surface of the leaf, this means that most of the stomata are located there.

Cones

Can you imagine what the world looked like 300 million years ago? One thing you may be able to picture is the trees. That's when cone-bearing trees, such as pine and spruce, developed. Although it was such a long time ago, these trees, called conifers, haven't changed much over the years. In fact, conifers are some of the most successful plants in the world. They can grow in very cold or dry areas like the Arctic or desert edge where other plants can't survive. Much of their success is due to their cones.

The hard scales on the outside of the cone help protect the seeds inside from bad weather, poor growing conditions and cone eaters. When the right time comes, the scales can open and release the seeds to the wind, giving them the best chance of survival.

Pining for cones

Take a look at a pine tree in the spring. The reddish-purple cones growing upright at the tips of the branches are the young female cones. Now find the small, soft yellowish male cones farther down the branches. The yellow, dust-like pollen is blown by the wind from the male to the female cones. Once the female cone has been pollinated, its scales harden and close over the developing seeds. The cone stalk starts to bend downwards and the cone turns green. By the time the seeds inside the cone are ripe, the cone has turned brown and is pointing down towards the ground. At this time, the cone scales shrink and open, releasing the winged seeds to the wind.

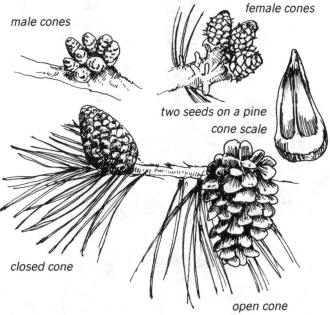

male cones

female cones

two seeds on a pine cone scale

closed cone

open cone

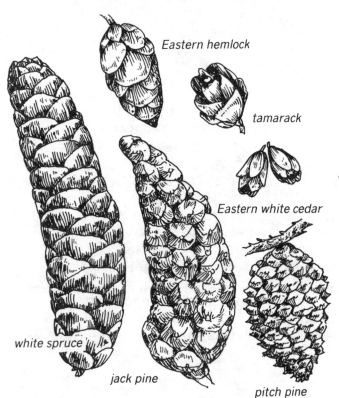

Eastern hemlock

tamarack

Eastern white cedar

white spruce

jack pine

pitch pine

In many kinds of conifers, the female cones form and ripen in the same year, but in pines it may take two or three years. You may be able to find cones at different stages of development on the same tree.

Cone magic

Conifer trees have survived so long because their cones are specially designed to open and close in order to protect or disperse their seeds at the right time.

You can make different cones open or close, like magic, by simulating the conditions that cones endure in nature.

You'll need:
5 jack pine or Scotch pine cones
a cookie sheet
an oven
2 dry, white pine or hemlock cones with open scales
a large bowl of water
a paper towel

1. Place one jack pine or Scotch pine cone on a cookie sheet and put it into an oven at 150°C (300°F) for 15 minutes. (Ask an adult to help you.) At the same time, place a cone of the same kind on a table for comparison.

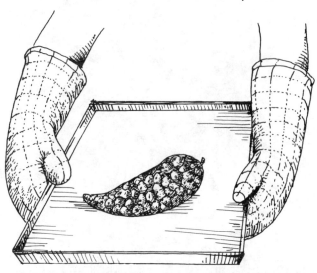

2. Check what has happened to the cone in the oven. Compare it to the cone on the table.

3. Try placing the other jack pine or Scotch pine cones in the oven, one at a time, at cooler or warmer temperatures to see what happens. You should find that a hot oven will make the cone open, releasing the seeds inside. The heat from the oven is doing what a forest fire in nature does. After a fire, jack pine seeds are released to the soil, where they can grow in the rich ashes of the burned wood, without any competition from larger trees. This helps them get a head start on other plants and helps the forest recover from the fire faster.

4. Place a white pine or hemlock cone in a bowl of water for 15 minutes. Leave the other cone dry for comparison.

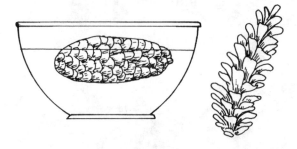

5. Check what has happened to the wet cone. You should find that the scales have started to close. The bowl of water represents a heavy rainstorm that could soak the cones. Since the seeds rely on wind to blow them to a new spot to grow, the seeds must be as light and dry as possible. In order to keep them dry, the scales close over the seeds during wet periods, acting like little umbrellas.

6. Take the wet cone out of the water and set it aside on a paper towel to dry. Watch what happens as the cone dries out.

Take a peek at a beak

Next time you visit the zoo, take a look at all the different kinds of beaks birds have. Each beak shape is designed for eating a certain type of food—fish, mammals, insects, fruit and nuts, or nectar. By looking at the shape of a bird's beak you can guess at its main food source and sometimes even its habitat (where it lives). Beaks are also important clues to help you identify birds. Try to match these birds' beaks with the food they eat. (Answers on page 158.)

Pelican
My scoop-like beak helps me trap slippery food. What do I eat?

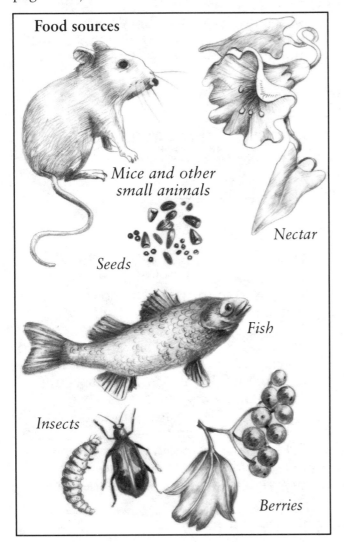

Food sources

Mice and other small animals

Seeds

Nectar

Fish

Insects

Berries

Hummingbird
My straw-like beak is perfect for poking into things and sucking up food. What do I eat?

Swift
My beak may be small and weak but it opens wide like a vacuum cleaner to help me catch food in mid-air. What do I eat?

Waxwing
My short, slightly hooked beak is great for picking things. What do I eat?

Cardinal
My thick, conical beak is terrific for crunching and cracking food. What do I eat?

Hawk
My strong, hooked beak can tear food apart. What do I eat?

Woodpecker wonders

You'd probably get a headache if you banged your head against a tree, but woodpeckers don't seem to mind. Their thick head bones act as shock absorbers while extra strong muscles in their head and neck help them work away at a tree for hours. That's not the only amazing thing about woodpeckers. Read on . . . .

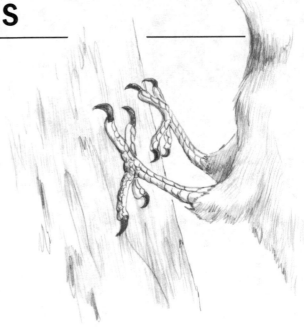

Stick out your tongue
Everyone notices the woodpecker's large, strong beak, but have you ever wondered about its tongue? Woodpeckers that eat insects have a tongue like a fishing lure. Barbed hooks along the sides hook into the insect and glue-like saliva finishes the job.

The tongue is attached to bones and elastic-like tissue stored in the woodpecker's head. When the tongue is needed to get at insects inside a tree hole, the whole system slides forward and the tongue shoots out. Fully extended, a woodpecker's tongue can reach up to five times farther than its beak!

Hanging on
How would you like to eat dinner while hanging from the trunk of a tree? Sound tricky? Not for a woodpecker. It has special "hanging on" gear. And best of all, its gear is built in.

The woodpecker has two toes pointed forward and two backward. The back toes, plus its sharp, curved claws, give it a good grip. For extra safety, it props itself up with its tail, which is made of extra stiff feathers.

What's that noise?
Woodpeckers usually tap on trees, but you may get one tapping on your drainpipe or tin roof. Why? Like little children, woodpeckers love to make noise. Since most woodpecker species don't sing like other birds, they tap in order to claim their breeding territory. The noisier the tapping the better the woodpecker likes it, and your drainpipe is a lot louder than a tree. Don't worry though—when it comes to feeding or chiselling out a nesting cavity, these birds stick to trees.

A hole hunt

Put on your detective hat and grab your binoculars. The woodpecker hole hunt is about to begin. Different woodpeckers make different sizes of feeding and nesting holes, as well as different hole patterns. Using their holes as clues, you can identify some of the species living in your area without even seeing them.

One woodpecker, the Yellow-bellied Sapsucker, drills several rows of small holes in live trees in woods and orchards. It feeds on the sap and small insects that collect in the holes.

The large Pileated Woodpecker can make holes big enough to put your whole fist in.

The Acorn Woodpecker, also called the California Woodpecker, stores acorns by drilling holes in tree trunks or poles and then stuffing in one acorn per hole. That's take-out food with a difference!

Owl prowl

Many species of owls are "nocturnal," or active at night, so the best time to prowl for owls is after dusk.

- Choose your spot carefully. Do some research to find out what kind of habitat various owls prefer. If you've seen an owl before, go back to that spot: you might get lucky again.
- Choose your time. Spring is a good time for your outing because owls are nesting and actively defending their territories.
- Look for owls perched in large trees near the edges of open fields and road sides where they hunt. If you hear an owl calling, move quickly and quietly towards the sound.
- Be patient and don't talk or rustle around. If you see an owl, the wait will have been worthwhile.

Owl pellets: nature's jigsaw puzzles

You wouldn't eat a chicken whole, bones and all. You'd spit out the bones and just eat the soft parts. Owls aren't so fussy. They gobble down small mice and voles whole in one gulp, but they can't digest the tough bits. Instead they spit them up in the form of pellets. By dissecting these little "packages" of bones, claws, beaks, teeth, fur and feathers, you can find clues about what an owl has been eating. Scientists use owl pellets to help figure out how owl diets change in different places and seasons and to guess at an owl's role in the local food chain.

Dissecting owl pellets

You don't need to be an expert to dissect an owl's pellet and try to figure out what the bird has been eating. Here's how to do it.

You'll need: owl pellets
Ziplock plastic bags
a dish of warm water
paper towels
tweezers or two skewers
field guides to mammals and
insects

1. Look for owl pellets at the foot of owls' daytime roosts and nests or under nighttime feeding perches.
2. Store them in a Ziplock plastic bag until you're ready to dissect them.

3. Small pellets can be dissected dry, but larger samples should be soaked for an hour or so in a dish of warm water.

4. Put the softened pellets on paper towels. Gently separate the hard parts (bones, teeth, etc.) from the soft parts (fur, feathers, etc.) using the tweezers or skewers.

5. Use a field guide to help you identify the different parts. Your most important clues will be the shape, size and teeth pattern of the skulls and the head parts, wings and legs of the insects.

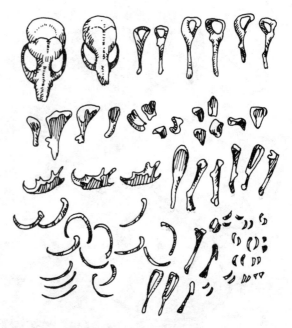

Bones you might find in an owl pellet

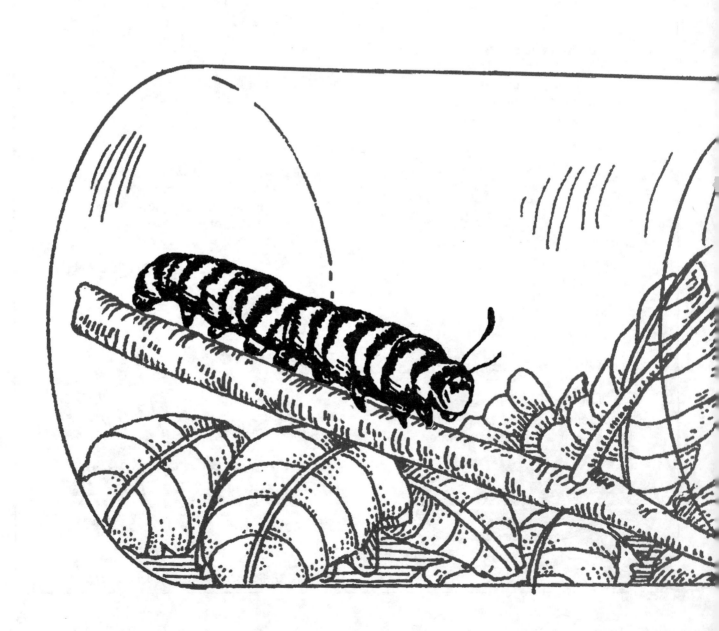

Indoor Adventures

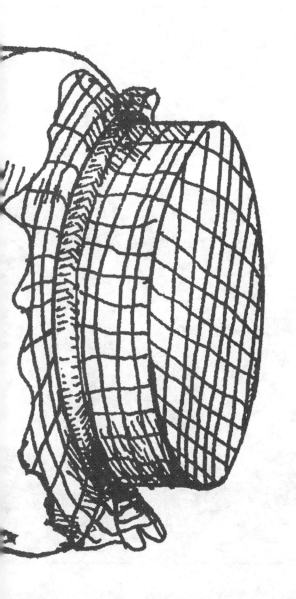

Bring a bit of nature indoors and discover the secret lives of some plants and animals that share your world. Set up a terrarium or ant palace and watch how the tiny creatures live. Raise a butterfly or moth and witness one of nature's miracles as caterpillars turn into adult insects. Plan an indoor bug hunt and discover why house flies can walk on the ceiling without falling. Grow plant pretzels or make a moss garden. Whatever the weather outside, you can have non-stop nature indoors.

Make a terrarium

Getting down on your hands and knees is a great way to find insects, especially in the woods. But when it's cold or wet you may not want to hang around very long. Instead, you can try to recreate a mini woodland habitat in your home by making a terrarium.

You'll need:

a large relish or pickle jar with a screen cover
pebbles or sand
small, untreated charcoal pieces
part of a rotting log
a trowel
soil dug from the woods, including leaf litter
water
some woodland plants and mosses from around the log
an elastic band

1. Turn your jar on its side. The jar's side is now the bottom of your terrarium.
2. Place a layer of small pebbles or sand on the bottom of your terrarium for drainage.

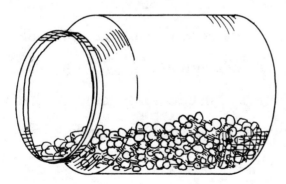

3. Sprinkle a thin layer of charcoal pieces over the sand to keep the soil fresh.

4. Take your terrarium to the woods and find a small rotting log, full of life. Remember, you can't dig in parks, conservation areas or nature reserves. If you're on private land, be sure to get permission first. Take only a few specimens so you don't disturb the area too much.
5. Add the soil and leaf litter from around the rotting log to your terrarium so that it is 5-7 cm (2-3 inches) thick.

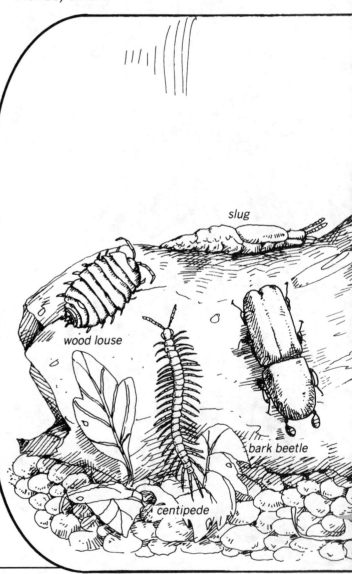

slug

wood louse

bark beetle

centipede

6. Moisten this mixture slightly and shape it into small hills to simulate the natural ups and downs of the forest floor.
7. Carefully break off a piece of the rotting log and place it in your terrarium. Take as large a piece as will fit, but don't squish it in.
8. Dig up some of the mosses and small woodland plants growing around the log. Place them in your terrarium as they grew in the wild. Press the plants down firmly and dampen them with water. Your terrarium should be kept moist but not soaked.
9. Place the screen over the jar mouth and secure it with the elastic band.
10. At home, place your container in an area where it will get some natural sunlight, fresh air and temperatures between 18 and 24°C (65 and 75°F). Avoid too much direct sunlight, dry heat or draughts. Place heavy objects, such as two big books, in front of and behind your terrarium to keep it from rolling.
11. When you're finished with your terrarium, be sure to return the creatures to their original homes when the weather is warm again.

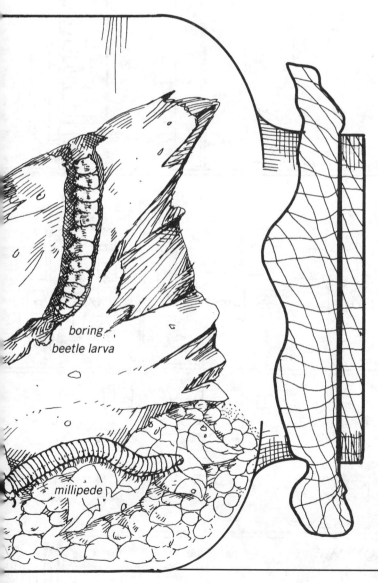

boring beetle larva

millipede

Take note
Keep a pencil and notebook near your terrarium so you can jot down interesting events. Try to make a list or sketch of all of the creatures you see. When looking at your mini-world, try to answer these questions:

☐ *What is the colour, size, shape, number of legs, etc. of each animal?*
☐ *Where do the different creatures live?*
☐ *Do they move around or stay in one place?*
☐ *How do they move?*
☐ *Are they more active at certain times of day or night?*
☐ *What do they eat?*
☐ *What do the animals use the plants and soil for?*

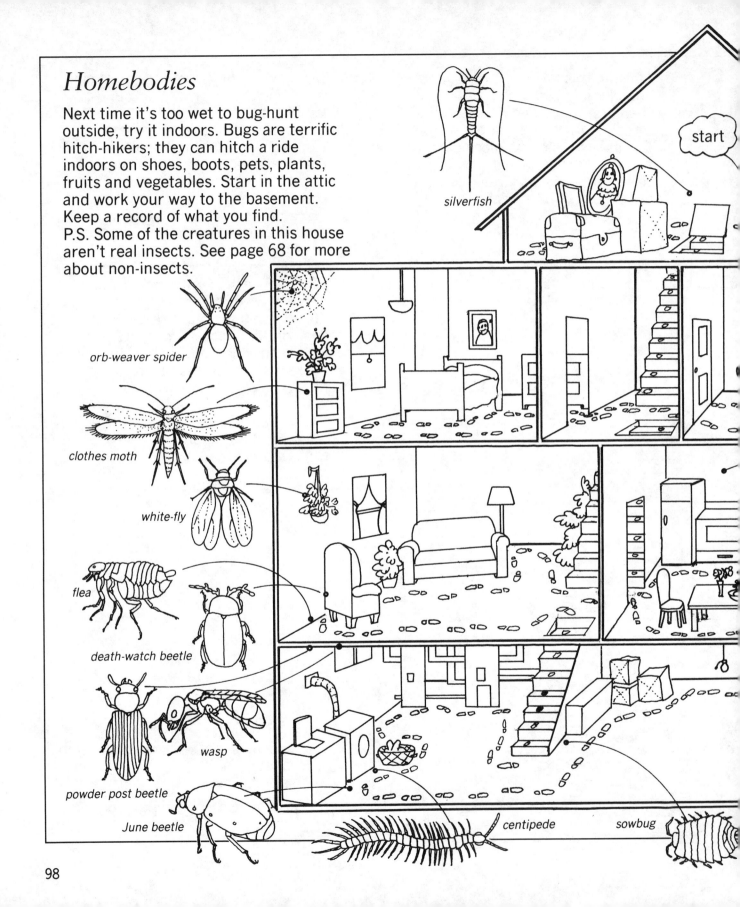

Homebodies

Next time it's too wet to bug-hunt outside, try it indoors. Bugs are terrific hitch-hikers; they can hitch a ride indoors on shoes, boots, pets, plants, fruits and vegetables. Start in the attic and work your way to the basement. Keep a record of what you find.
P.S. Some of the creatures in this house aren't real insects. See page 68 for more about non-insects.

start

silverfish

orb-weaver spider

clothes moth

white-fly

flea

death-watch beetle

powder post beetle

wasp

June beetle

centipede

sowbug

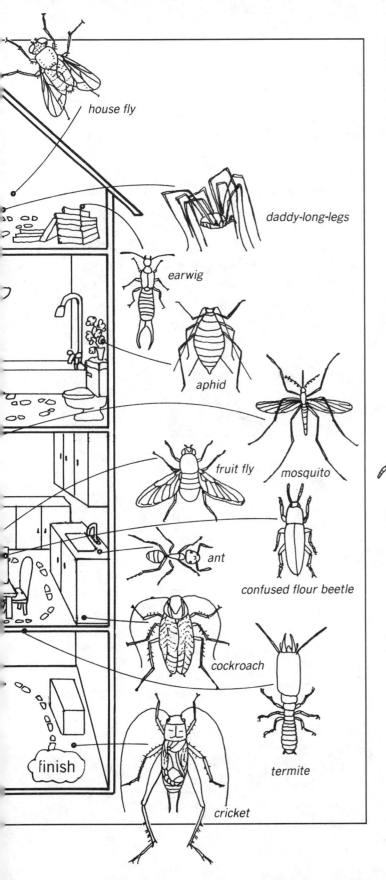

house fly

daddy-long-legs

earwig

aphid

mosquito

fruit fly

confused flour beetle

ant

cockroach

termite

cricket

finish

Bug off!
Tired of swatting and missing? Try some of these unusual ways to get bugs to bug off.

☐ Hang sprigs of mint in doorways to keep flies out.
☐ Catch a few ladybugs and put them on your houseplants to control aphids.
☐ Grow tansy outside your kitchen wall to keep ants away.
☐ Encourage toads in your garden. One toad can eat up to 10 000 insects in just three months. In fact, before insect sprays were invented, some people kept toads indoors to control bugs.

☐ Grow insect-repelling plants, such as marigolds, asters, chrysanthemums, nasturtiums, cosmos, coreopsis and coriander.
☐ Attract insect-eating birds to your garden by providing birdhouses, bird baths, shrubs and trees for shelter.

Flies inside

"Buzz, buzz, thwack, buzz, buzz." Can you guess what that is? It's the familiar sound of a frustrated house fly caught inside a window. When the warm weather arrives, house flies that have spent the winter in your walls or attic try to make their escape. Most people are only too happy to see them go. Before you say goodbye, look for these nifty fly features.

Neat feet

Have you ever wondered how flies walk upside-down on the ceiling without falling off? Each of their six feet is specially equipped with a pair of small claws that helps them cling to rough surfaces. But, how do flies walk on smooth glass? Under each claw are two tiny pads covered in hairs that release a glue-like substance so flies can stick to glass or ceilings without tumbling down.

Flies flying

Flies are great fliers. House flies beat their wings 11 000 times per minute and can fly an average speed of 8 km/h (5 mph). It's the fast wing beats that produce the buzzing sound you hear when a fly flies by. Unlike butterflies or dragonflies, flies have only one pair of wings. Instead of hind wings, they have little rods called halteres on their thorax that act as stabilizers during flight and keep them flying level.

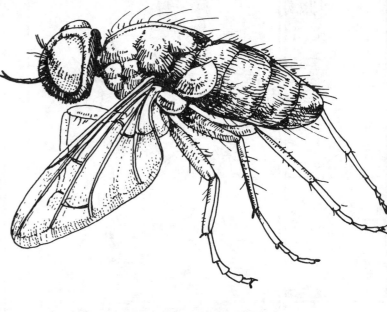

Have you ever noticed the little black lines all over a fly's wings? These are veins. Just as your veins carry blood to various parts of your body, the fly's veins take blood to its wings, but they also do other things. When the adult emerges from its pupa, air is pumped through the veins to help the folded wings expand. The veins also strengthen the wings and provide support, just as the cross-pieces on a kite keep the kite from collapsing.

A fly's eyes

If you held a colander up to your face and looked through it, you'd see many tiny holes aimed in slightly different directions. This is just what the compound eyes of flies and other insects are like. Instead of having only one lens in each eye, like you, each house fly's eye has 4000 tiny lenses in individual six-sided facets. Each facet is like each hole in the colander— pointing at a slightly different angle and seeing a small part of a total picture. When all of the tiny parts are put together, the insect sees a

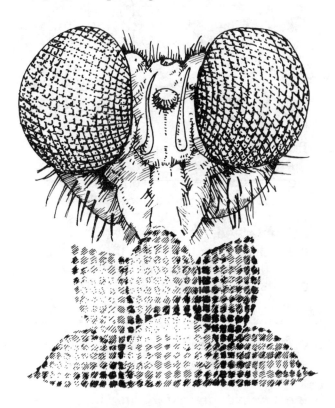

mosaic-like image. The more facets, the clearer the picture. Although compound eyes sound like super seers, they don't work as well as your eyes. Insects can't focus their eyes so, although they can see movement very well, images are not clear beyond 1 m (2-3 feet). And with no eyelids, insects have to keep their eyes open day and night—even when they sleep.

"Flies in the sugar-bowl, two by two . . ."

The flies in your sugar-bowl aren't "skipping to my Lou," they're probably tasting the sugar— with their feet! Can you imagine wading barefoot across a pizza? A fly can tell if food is worth eating, just by walking on it. But since a fly's mouth is designed only to soak up liquids, it can't just eat your sugar. First, it spits saliva onto it to make the food liquidy, and then it sucks up the sweet treat like a sponge.

Fly facts

- [ ] *The expression "breeding like flies" comes from flies' fantastic ability to multiply. Each female house fly produces about 1000 eggs in only a few weeks.*

- [ ] *Don't let the combing and cleaning routine of the fly on your table fool you. A single house fly can carry millions of germs inside and outside of its body.*

Raising a monarch butterfly

When you were born, you looked like a very small version of the person you are today. But most insects start out life looking completely different from their adult form. Monarch butterflies, for example, go through four different stages during their metamorphosis (met-a-more-foe-sis), or period of "growing up." These are the egg, larva, pupa and adult stages. You can raise your own monarch butterfly and watch the whole process, from egg or caterpillar to adult in a little over a month. Monarch butterflies are easy to raise and beautiful to watch.

You'll need:
monarch butterfly eggs or caterpillars
  (2 or 3)
fresh milkweed plants daily
a small container of water
a large clear jar (1 L [1 quart] or more)
a long stick
cheesecloth or fine screening
an elastic

1. Pick part of a milkweed plant that has monarch eggs or caterpillars on it. Bring the plant and insect home and put the milkweed stem in a container of cool water to keep it from wilting. Extra milkweed leaves can be brought home at the same time and stored in water in the fridge for two to three days. This saves you a daily trip to the milkweed patch for caterpillar food.

2. Place a stick in the jar for the caterpillars to crawl on. Cover the jar's opening with cheesecloth or fine screening and secure it with an elastic. You must supply fresh milkweed leaves daily for your caterpillars to eat.

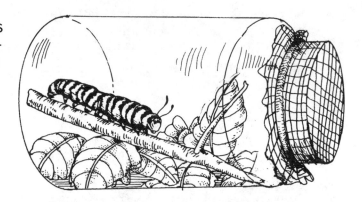

3. Take notes and/or photographs of the various stages in your butterfly's life. They will help you remember the experience and share it with others.
4. When the adult monarch butterfly has emerged, let it go free so that it may carry on with its life. If possible, it should be released where the original eggs or caterpillars were found.

How to find monarch eggs and caterpillars
June and early July are the best times to search for monarch eggs or caterpillars. Visit open fields or roadsides to find milkweed plants. Their large, pinkish blossoms smell beautiful and are easy to spot. Check under the milkweed's leaves for the tiny bun-shaped eggs. Or you may find the yellow, white and black striped caterpillars climbing on the stems or leaves. The bigger the caterpillar, the sooner it will turn into a chrysalis.

What you'll see:

Week 1:
Monarch butterfly eggs hatch in four to five days, producing a tiny yellow, black and white striped caterpillar. This is the monarch's larva stage. The caterpillar eats constantly and grows rapidly. As it grows, it sheds its skin to make more room.

Week 2:
At age two weeks your caterpillar is 2700 times its original size! Imagine what would happen if you grew that much? Watch out, Jolly Green Giant!

Week 3:
The caterpillar spins a silk pad on a leaf or branch. It attaches itself to the pad and hangs upside down. The larva's striped skin will gradually change into the emerald green case of the pupa, called a chrysalis. Inside this case the adult starts to form.

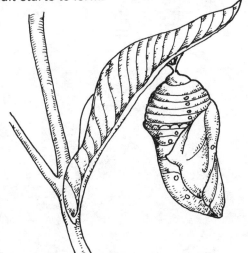

Week 4:
Within nine or ten days, the green coloured chrysalis fades, leaving a see-through pupal case. Through this "window" you will spy the bright orange and black folded wings of the adult, almost ready to come out.

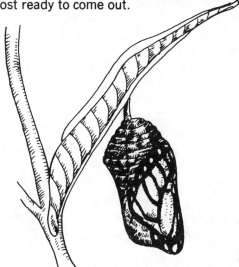

Week 5:
About two weeks after the chrysalis is formed, the adult butterfly splits it open and climbs out head first.

Buried treasures

Have you ever wondered where all the moths go in the fall, or where they come from in the summer? Like many animals, moths hibernate—but not in caves like bats. Moths spend the winter inside cocoons. Moths have a cycle similar to that of butterflies. They go through four different stages:

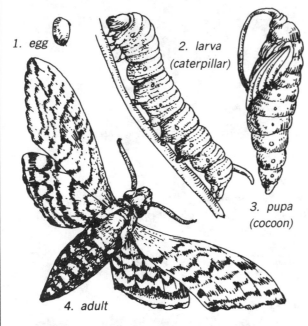

1. egg
2. larva (caterpillar)
3. pupa (cocoon)
4. adult

In the summer, adults lay their eggs which hatch into caterpillars within a few weeks. Caterpillars spend their summer doing nothing but eating. In the fall, many moth caterpillars dig into the ground and form pupae. The earth keeps them warm during winter and hides them from hungry birds and mice. Finally, in the spring, they transform into adults.

With a few materials, you can collect some pupae in late winter and watch them transform into adults in late spring. It's like digging for buried treasure and then waiting to see the jewels inside.

You'll need:
a trowel
a rinsed-out plastic tub (margarine or yoghurt) lined with cotton batting or shredded newspaper
earth or vermiculite (available at most garden stores)
water
window screening 25-30 cm (10-12 inches) wide
scissors
tape
a stick, pencil-thick, about 25 cm (10 inches) long
a foil pie plate

1. When the ground has thawed, find a tree in the open (poplar, birch, willow, beech or ash) and dig around the roots. Many pupae prefer sandy loam soil, so avoid areas with clay, stony or mucky ground. Dig about 15 cm (6 inches) down, 20-25 cm (8-10 inches) away from the north side of the tree. You should also check for pupae under any loose bark near the base of the tree and search carefully through the grass roots.
2. When you've found two or three pupae, gently place them in your lined container and carefully take them home.

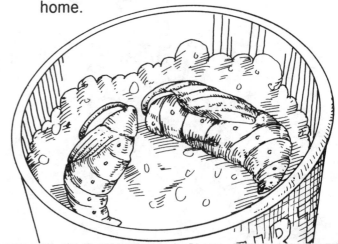

3. Cover the pupae with 3 cm (1-2 inches) of sterilized earth or vermiculite and put them in a cool place, such as a basement. (To sterilize the earth, place it on a cookie sheet in a 176°C [350°F] oven for 20 minutes.)

4. Sprinkle the soil lightly with water twice a week.

5. In late spring, check your pupae for signs of movement and changes in appearance, such as change of colour, or splitting of the pupa's skin. These are signals that the adults are ready to emerge.

6. Now roll the screen into a tube and cut it so that it stands up just on the inside edge of your container. Tape the side closed. Place the stick upright in the container and lay a pie plate over the top, to form a cage as shown.

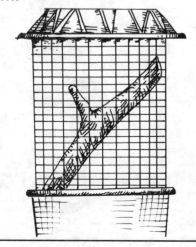

7. Keep a close eye on your treasures and you can witness one of nature's miracles. Watch as the pupa's skin splits along the back, allowing the adult to slowly climb out.

8. The adult moths will climb onto the stick and dry their wings. Inside the cocoon, the wings were tightly folded. But now that the adult can have a stretch, it pumps body fluids into the wings, making them expand into moth-size wings for flying. After a day, let your moths go free. You can keep the cocoon case as part of a collection or display.

Tricks of the trade
Nature photographers sometimes raise their own moths and butterflies. In the wild, adult insects sometimes have damaged wings or other body parts but "home-grown" specimens are usually perfect for pictures. Besides, the photographer doesn't have to search for a moth in the wild or wait hours for it to set down so a picture can be taken. Why not try photographing your pupa and adult?

An ant palace

If you could shrink down to ant-size and follow an ant into its home, you'd find a palace below the ground. The palace is ruled by a queen ant who is surrounded by thousands of servants (workers). Ant homes have lots of different rooms for eggs, larvae and pupae, pantries for food and even special rooms for their garbage. You can set up a mini-ant palace in your own home and see for yourself what goes on underground.

You'll need:
a large glass jar
soft, garden soil
a trowel
cheesecloth
an elastic band
tape
black paper
food for ants—sugar, honey, bread
  crumbs

1. Fill your jar with loosely packed soil, leaving 5 or 6 cm (2 or 3 inches) of space at the top.
2. Look for a colony of small black or brown ants in an open area like a roadside, backyard, driveway or sidewalk crack. Dig the ants up with your trowel. Try to find the biggest ant, the queen, and put her in your jar along with as many workers as you can get.

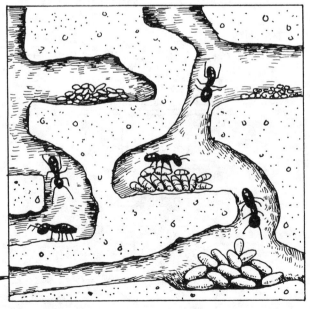

3. Secure the cheesecloth over the top of the jar with the elastic band.
4. Tape a piece of black paper around your jar up to the level of the earth.
5. To feed your ants, just sprinkle a little bit of sugar, honey and bread crumbs on top of the earth daily.
6. The ants will make a new colony and dig tunnels through the earth. The black paper encourages ants to dig right next to the glass. Remove the black paper for a short time every few days or so and peek in.
7. When you've finished watching your ant palace, return the ants to where you found them.

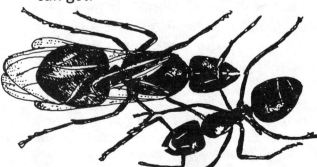

Amazing ant stories

☐ *Had an ant bath lately? Birds often let ants crawl all over them to help get them clean. The ants produce a chemical that kills lice and other tiny pests that live on birds.*

☐ *If you climb trees, keep a look out for ants. Dr. Edward O. Wilson found 43 species of ants on one tree in the Peruvian rain forest!*

☐ *Ever seen ants carrying a dead ant and wondered what they're doing? The corpses of ants give off special identifying odours that help workers know if the dead ant was a member of their colony. If it was, the pall-bearing ants carry their dead buddy off to the ant morgue—a special area that's like a compost heap.*

☐ *Ants communicate by using smells instead of sounds. Their bodies contain many different chemicals, each with its own odour and meaning. In their jaws, ants carry a chemical that signals an alarm, or call to war. If an ant's head is crushed accidentally, say by a person stepping on it, the alarm chemical is released and all the ants nearby get the message that a war has been declared. Ant soldiers will suddenly appear, ready to fight.*

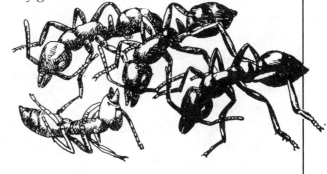

☐ *Ants are smart. How do we know? A researcher built special mazes for testing some ants. The ants had to find their way from their nest to a dish of food by travelling through the maze of corridors. After doing it once, the ants simply followed their scent trail. But even when the scent trail was removed, the ants could still get through the maze, proving that they memorized the correct path.*

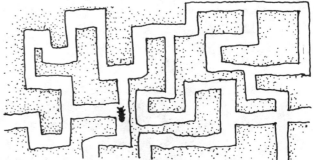

Nature's recyclers

Everyone's recycling these days. It may be a new idea for people, but nature has been doing it ever since life on earth began. In fact, there are millions of tiny plants and animals that spend their lives breaking down dead plants and animals into reusable nutrients. Without these well-hidden workers, our forests and meadows couldn't grow. With some simple equipment, you can discover some of these recyclers in a small sample of soil.

You'll need:
a shovel
some soil and leaf litter from the woods
a plastic bag
wire cutters
stiff wire screening with large holes
a funnel
a damp paper towel
a wide-mouth jar
a light
tweezers
a small magnifying glass

1. Use the shovel to dig up some leaf litter and soil and put it in the plastic bag.

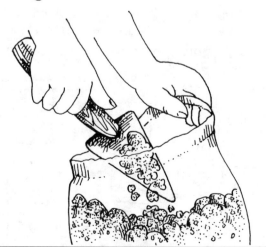

2. At home, set up your equipment. Cut the screen to fit inside the funnel, about 6 cm (2 inches) from the mouth. Place the damp paper towel in the bottom of your jar and set the funnel in the open end of the jar. Place your light so that it shines directly over the funnel.

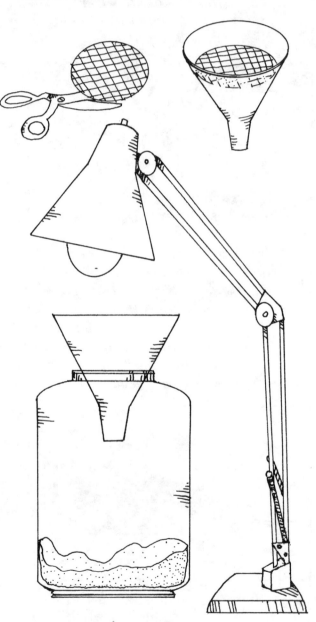

3. Put the soil in your funnel and turn on the light. The rest of the room should be dark.

4. Leave the equipment set up overnight. The creatures in your sample will try to get away from the heat and light of your lamp by burrowing deeper into the soil. Eventually they will fall through the funnel, into the jar below.

5. Gently pick up each creature with the tweezers so you can get a closer look with your magnifying glass.

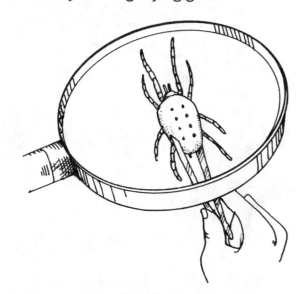

6. When you've finished, return the animals and soil to their habitat.

What you'll find

You'll probably find a variety of insects and non-insects in your soil. Here are a few to look for:

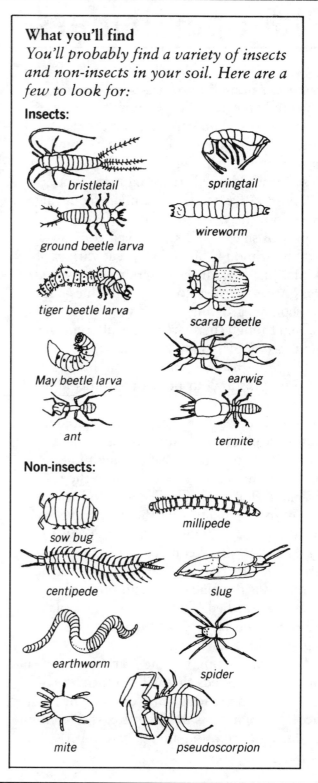

Insects:

bristletail

springtail

ground beetle larva

wireworm

tiger beetle larva

scarab beetle

May beetle larva

earwig

ant

termite

Non-insects:

sow bug

millipede

centipede

slug

earthworm

spider

mite

pseudoscorpion

Plant particulars

Hundreds of millions of years ago, plants appeared on earth. They're now the most widespread and numerous living things. Whether you like your plants big or small, nature's got something for you. From the giant west-coast redwoods reaching more than 105 m (345 feet) tall, to the microscopic algae in a pond, the world of plants offers an endless display of shapes and sizes. Even your own neighbourhood is home to a great variety of plants. Just look at the differences between the grass, trees, garden flowers, vegetables and houseplants growing around you.

Even though there are many different sizes and types of plants, all plants have the same basic parts. Just as your heart and lungs are major organs in your body that you couldn't live without, plants also have organs that they couldn't live without. The three essential parts that most plants have are roots, stem and leaves. The roots anchor the plant and take up water and minerals from the soil to the rest of the plant. The stem acts like a main highway system for the plant—it's the busy travel route for water and minerals going from roots to leaves and for food coming from leaves to the rest of the plant. The stem also supports the plant and is the place where all other plant parts are attached. The green leaf of a plant is a mini food factory for the plant (see page 78).

The flowering part of the plant is responsible for producing seeds that will, in turn, create new plants in the following season. The key to success in plants, as in all nature, is to continue producing generation after generation.

Searching for sun

You need nutritious food and water in order to stay healthy and grow. Plants also need food (minerals) and water, but another important ingredient is sunlight. This activity will help you see just how far a plant will go — or grow — in order to reach sunlight.

You'll need:
2 sheets of heavy black paper
a fast-growing plant, like a bean seedling planted in a pot
sticky tape
scissors
water

1. Roll one sheet of paper into a tube large enough to fit around the potted plant. Tape the sides together securely and set the roll of paper aside.
2. When your seedling is 3 to 4 cm (1 to 2 inches) high, place the tube of paper over the pot. Cut your tube so that it is a few centimetres (1 inch) higher than your plant.

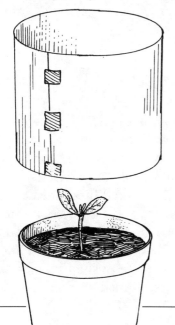

3. Cut a piece of black paper to make a lid that will lie flat over the top of your tube. Towards one edge of the lid, cut a hole about 2 cm (1 inch) wide as shown.

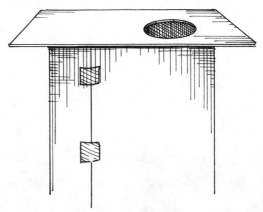

4. Place your plant, in its tube, in front of a bright window. Remember to water the plant.
5. The plant inside the tube will be growing in the dark. It will react to the small circle of light let in by the hole in the lid and will grow towards it. Once you see the plant poking through the hole, remove the black paper and look at the shape of your plant. You will find that the stem has grown long, spindly and crooked, stretching for the light.

Sowing seeds

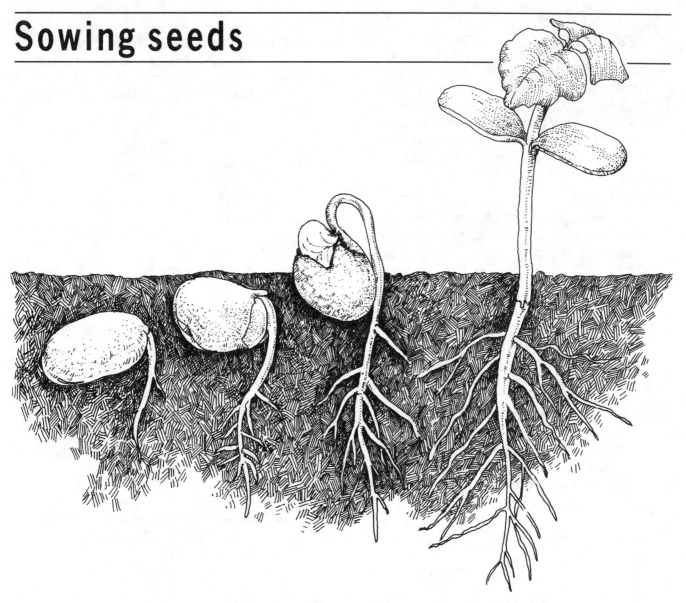

If you've ever planted seeds, you know how exciting it is when you see the first signs that your plants are growing. You may notice a little bump in the soil and then some cracking of the soil surface. The tiny shoot from your seed is pushing its way up through the soil to reach the open air and sunlight. Have you ever wondered how your seeds have the strength to move soil or what happens after you plant the seed to turn it into a growing plant?

Like a sponge, your seed soaks up water. As the water is absorbed, the contents of the seed swell and swell until they crack the seed coat (outer shell of the seed). Inside the seed, the root and shoot cells have stretched with all the water they've soaked up, and they are now free to grow out from the seed coat and push through the soil. This process is called germination. As the cells stretch and multiply, the plant parts are pushed further and further through the soil until you see the shoot poking up into the air.

Bursting beans

Find out how mung beans turn into mighty beans and blow their cork as they germinate.

You'll need:
a clear plastic jar with a cork stopper
  (available at craft stores)
fresh mung beans (available in grocery
  stores)
water
a plastic bag
a twist tie

1. Fill the jar with mung beans and add water until it reaches the top of the beans.
2. Put the cork firmly in the mouth of the jar.
3. Place the jar in a plastic bag tied with a twist tie and put the bag in a dark cupboard for 3 to 4 days.
4. Check the jar. You should find that the cork has been pushed out of the jar by the pressure of the growing beans inside.
5. Notice the level of water in the jar now. The beans have absorbed the water and swelled. Inside each bean, the root and shoot cells have taken in water and started to stretch. It is these stretching cells that eventually burst from the seed and push through soil.

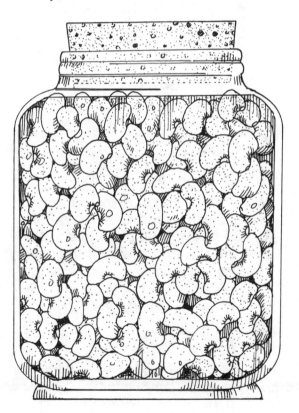

Putting down roots

How can you turn one plant into two or turn part of your lunch into a plant? It may sound like magic, but all you need to do is grow some roots. Try these simple tricks for rooting plants and you can expand your collection of houseplants in no time.

To root a cutting **you'll need**:
a sharp knife
a geranium
a flower pot
potting soil
water
a plastic bag
an elastic

1. Cut a 15 cm (6 inch) shoot (branch) from a geranium plant, near a joint where a leaf meets the stem.

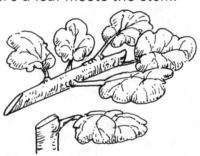

2. Pull off the lowest couple of leaves. Plant the shoot in a pot of potting soil so that about half of the shoot is buried.

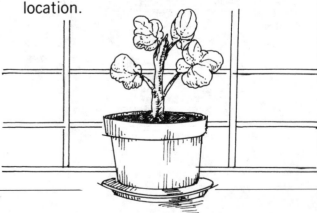

3. Water the soil and place a plastic bag over the pot and plant, to keep moisture in. Close the open end of the bag with an elastic.

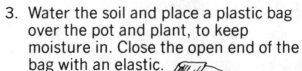

4. Leave the plant in a shaded spot for two or three weeks. To check whether the roots have grown, gently tug on the stem. If the cutting doesn't slip out easily, then it has rooted.

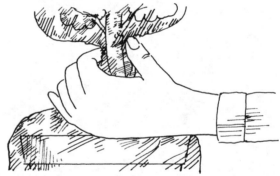

5. When the cutting has rooted, remove the plastic bag and keep the pot in the shade until the plant begins to grow well. Then transfer it to a sunny location.

Growing garbage

If you've eaten an avocado for lunch, instead of throwing out the huge pit inside, save it to start another avocado plant. You can grow carrot plants by cutting off and saving the top few centimetres (inch) of an unpeeled carrot. Or if you come across a potato that has already sprouted little white "eyes," put it aside and use it to grow a potato plant indoors.

You'll need:
an avocado pit, carrot top or sprouted
   potato
a glass
water
toothpicks
plant pots
potting soil

1. Any of the above plant parts can be rooted in the same way. Fill the jar with water.
2. Stick some toothpicks into the avocado pit, and rest it on the rim of the jar as shown. The bottom of the pit should be in water.

3. Place the jar on a window sill. Keep the water level high so that the lower part of the pit is always in water.
4. In a few weeks, you should see the pit split and a root emerge from the bottom. Shortly afterwards, a shoot (stem) will begin to grow upwards from the pit. When the plant sprouts its first leaves, remove the toothpicks and carefully transfer the pit to a pot containing soil. Be very careful not to disturb the root. Place your plant near a sunny window.

Growing with gravity

If you plant a seed or a bulb upside-down in the ground, will the roots grow up through the soil and the stem grow down underground? The answer is always no. No matter how you do your planting, the stem will always grow up and the roots will always grow down. How does the plant know which way is up? The plant is responding to the earth's gravitational pull — a reaction called geotropism. Gravity causes the plant's growth hormone, called auxin, to collect on the underside of the root and shoot. The root and shoot cells, however, react differently to the auxin. In the shoot, the auxin stimulates growth and causes the underside of the shoot to grow more rapidly, thus raising the shoot up. However, auxin has the reverse effect in the root. The auxin inhibits growth on the underside of the root, thus causing the top side to grow more rapidly, sending the root downwards.

What would happen if astronauts took plants up in space where there is no gravity? Experiments have shown that when gravity does not direct the growth of a plant, the roots and shoots will grow any which way.

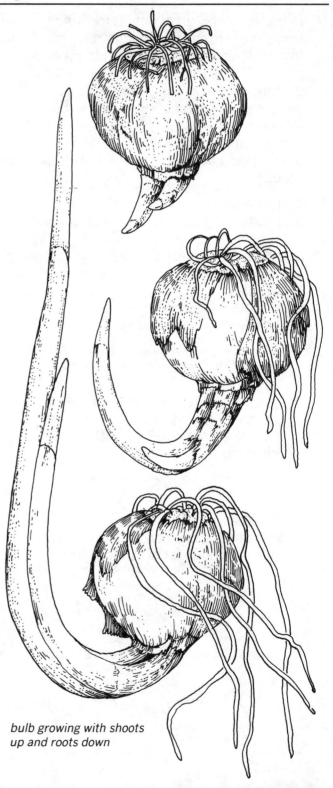

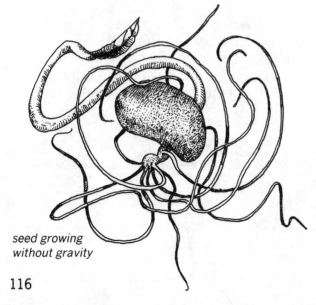

seed growing
without gravity

bulb growing with shoots
up and roots down

116

Plant pretzels

You can see geotropism in action for yourself by planting some radish seeds and turning them into wild-looking plants.

You'll need:
10 radish seeds
water
a glass jar
wet paper towels

1. Soak your radish seeds in water for a few hours.
2. Line your glass jar with wet paper towels.
3. Slide your seeds between the paper towels and the glass, so that you can see them.

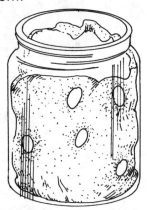

4. Put your jar in a dark cupboard until the seeds have sprouted and the stem is about 3 cm (1 inch) long.

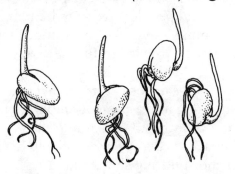

5. Pour off any extra water from the jar and turn the jar on its side. Keep the jar in the dark so that your stem's growth is not affected by the direction of light.

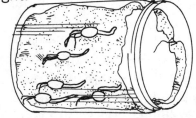

6. After one day, look at the roots and stems. In what direction are they growing?
7. Turn your jar right side up again and make sure the paper towels are still wet. Leave the jar in the dark for another day.

8. Check the roots and stems again. Are they still growing in the same direction or have they changed? You should find that no matter what position your jar is in, the stems will always grow up and the roots will always grow down. By changing the jar's position, you have made gravity turn the plant this way and that.

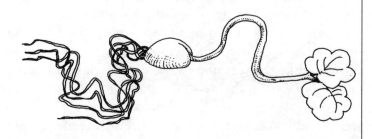

Masses of mosses

If you got down on your hands and knees with a magnifying glass, you could enter the world of mosses. You'd find yourself among mosses that look like palm trees, pine trees, ferns and even feathers. Mosses grow in all these forms and many more—there are more than 20 000 different kinds of mosses. Most mosses grow on land—on soil, trees, rocks or rotting logs—but some moss species can be found underwater in freshwater streams and ponds. Mosses are found everywhere in the world except deserts, so you're bound to come across some in the woods or even in the crack of a city sidewalk. Unlike most plants, green mosses can even thrive beneath a blanket of snow in the winter.

At first glance, you might think all mosses look alike, but that would be like saying all plants look alike. Although mosses share some general characteristics, such as stems, undivided leaves and no roots (they have hair-like parts called rhizoids that function like roots instead), the similarities end there. A close-up look at different kinds of mosses reveals an amazing assortment of size, shape, colour, texture and arrangement of leaves, stems and spore capsules (flower-like pods on thin stalks). Mosses can also change their appearance depending on how wet or dry the growing conditions are.

Get out your magnifying glass and take a look at a sample of dry moss and a sample of wet moss. You'll notice that the leaves of the dried moss are curled up, twisted and grey or brown while the wet moss's leaves are flat and green. Now drop the dry moss into a glass of water. What happens? You should see the stems and leaves straighten out and the green

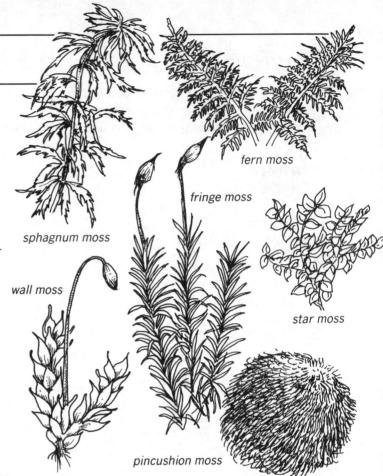

sphagnum moss

fern moss

fringe moss

wall moss

star moss

pincushion moss

colour return. This is what happens to moss in the wild when there is a dry spell followed by rain. Mosses have an amazing ability to "come back to life."

These hardy plants have been important pioneers on near-bare landscapes. Mosses can grow in very shallow soils, creating thicker mats where larger plants can grow. Mosses also provide food for a great variety of animals, and people have found a number of uses for mosses over the years, too. Pioneers mixed moss with clay to fill the cracks in their log cabins. Laplanders even stuffed pillows with moss. Peat, formed from layers of decomposing mosses, is cut and dried for fuel in many countries. Garden nurseries also use peat moss for conditioning soil and keeping plants moist during shipping.

Plant a moss garden

You can start your own moss garden indoors and get to know these fascinating little plants even better.

You'll need:
moss
a knife
a bag
newspaper
a large, wide-mouth glass jar (4 L
  [4 quarts] or more) with lid
peat (available at a garden store)
potting soil
cheesecloth
water
a plant mister
stones or small ornaments (optional)

1. Find some different kinds of mosses growing on rocks, wood or soil. Cut a few shallow squares of moss and bring it home in a bag.

2. Place the moss between sheets of newspaper and leave it to dry for a few days in a warm, dry place.
3. Crumble the old soil away, until just the leafy moss remains. This moss will become the source for your new mosses.
4. Fill your jar half full with an equal mixture of peat and potting soil.
5. Put a layer of cheesecloth over the soil mixture and sprinkle the dried moss on top.

6. Cover with another layer of cheesecloth, and water thoroughly with the plant mister. Always keep the cheesecloth moist.

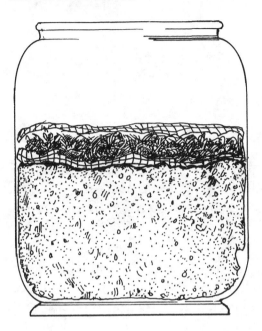

7. Put the lid on the jar and place it in a warm, shady spot. Your moss should start to grow in 6 to 8 weeks.
8. Keep your jar out of direct sunlight. Because it has a lid on, moisture should circulate within the jar and keep the moss damp.
9. Add some interesting stones or small ornaments to your jar to create a miniature landscape.

Falling for autumn

If you live where there are cold winters, you know that a sure sign that winter's coming is the colour change of the leaves on the trees. Why do leaves suddenly change colour? In most cases, the new colours, such as orange and yellow, have actually been in the leaves throughout the year, but they were hidden by the dominant green colour of chlorophyll. Some colours, though, such as reds, aren't produced until the fall. In the fall, the tree prepares for a rest. It will not grow during the winter because of the cold temperatures and lack of water. Part of the tree's preparation for winter involves stopping photosynthesis. First the chlorophyll in the leaves breaks down and when the green colouring breaks down, the other colours can be seen.

Once the leaf colours have brightened up the landscape, it will soon be time to get out the rake as the leaves begin to fall. Only certain types of trees, called deciduous, shed all their leaves at once. Oaks, maples, poplars and hickories are all deciduous trees. Where you live, the annual dropping of leaves likely occurs in the cool days of autumn. But even in tropical areas or climates with wet and dry seasons, deciduous trees lose their leaves at the start of the dry season.

Why do trees get rid of their leaves? The main reason is to conserve water. In cold winters, for example, the ground is frozen and it is very difficult for the roots to soak up water. So the tree has to stop using as much water as possible. Since leaves use up and release a lot of water, especially during photosynthesis, the leaves have to go. As autumn approaches, cells at the base of each leaf's stem die and form a barrier that blocks the flow of food and water between the leaf and the tree. This, along with the breakdown of chlorophyll in the leaf, kills the leaf. Once the chlorophyll is gone, the leaf can't photosynthesize any more. Eventually, the leaf can't hold on to the twig any longer and falls to the ground. The tree remains inactive through the winter until spring, when the buds open and the new leaves grow and start to photosynthesize again.

Uncovering colours

Each year the trees treat us to a show of the beautiful oranges and yellows of autumn leaves. You can uncover the hidden colours in green leaves with this simple version of paper chromatography that helps you separate the different pigments (colours) in a leaf.

You'll need:
a few green leaves
a glass jar
rubbing alcohol
a metal spoon
a 4 cm x 9 cm (2 inch x 4 inch) strip of coffee filter paper
sticky tape
a pencil
a piece of plain white paper

1. Tear your leaves into tiny pieces and put them in the jar.
2. Cover the leaves with rubbing alcohol. Caution: This liquid is poisonous, so do not taste it and avoid inhaling the fumes. Ask an adult to help you.
3. Mash the leaves up with the spoon and leave the mixture for 5 minutes.

4. Lower one end of the filter strip into the jar so that it just reaches the liquid inside. Tape the other end to your pencil and lay the pencil across the open jar mouth as shown.

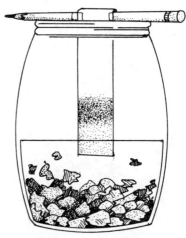

5. Watch as the liquid moves up the filter strip. When it is about half-way up, remove the strip and lay it on some clean paper to dry.
6. When the filter strip is dry, notice the bands of colour on it. You should see a green band, left by the chlorophyll pigment and a yellow or orange band left by a pigment called a carotenoid. The rubbing alcohol separated the pigments from the leaf mixture, and the filter paper absorbed both pigments and rubbing alcohol.
7. Try the same activity with leaves that have already turned colour.

How does it work?
The pigments, or colours, of the leaves were dissolved in the solution and then reabsorbed onto the filter paper. Since each pigment travelled on the paper at a different rate, each dried at a different location along the strip of paper. The result is a series of coloured bands, each representing one of the leaf's pigments.

Nature and You

From the time you get up in the morning until you go to bed at night, nature is an important part of your life. The food you eat, the paper you write on, the wood in your home, and some of your clothes and medicines are all products of nature. Get to know the nature around you better by attracting some birds to your yard or by going on a bug hunt. Find out why biting and stinging insects "bug" you, and try some home remedies to relieve the itch. Make your own maple syrup or boil up some plants to make natural dyes. Nature may seem never ending, but some species are endangered. Read on to find out how you can help them.

Make a bug catcher

What do you get when you cross a baby-food jar with two drinking straws? A terrific bug catcher, of course!

You'll need:
a hammer
a large nail
a jar lid
2 flexible bendable drinking straws or pieces of plastic aquarium tubing
tape
a small piece of cheesecloth
a small glass jar, like a baby-food jar

1. Hammer the nail into the lid to make two holes, 0.5 cm (¼ inch) wide each, and about 3 cm (1 inch) apart.
2. Turn the lid over and hammer down the sharp edges around the holes.
3. Push the two straws or tubes through the holes in the jar lid. Use tape, to seal around them.
4. Tape a piece of cheesecloth over the bottom of one tube. This is to prevent you sucking insects into your mouth.
5. Place the lid tightly on the jar.
6. To catch a bug, place the tube with the cheesecloth attached at the bottom in your mouth and suck hard. Place the open end of the other tube near a small insect. The insect will be sucked through the tube and into your jar. Now you can have a good look at it before letting it go.

Make a bug hat

For really buggy days, keep the flies out of your face with this easy-to-make bug hat.

You'll need:
mosquito netting
a hat
a needle
thread
scissors

1. Cut a length of mosquito netting wide enough to extend around the brim of your hat plus 5 cm (2 inches) extra, and about 35 cm (14 inches) long.
2. Sew the ends of your netting together with a 3 cm (1 inch) seam to form a tube.
3. Sew one end of the tube to the brim of your hat. Your stitches should be close together so there are no gaps where insects can sneak in.
4. Put on your hat and tuck the free end of the netting into the collar of your shirt.

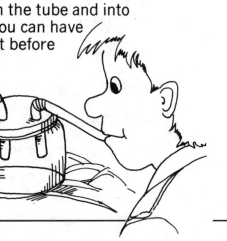

Make a binocular poncho

There's nothing worse than being rained on when you're out birdwatching. Your feet get wet, your head gets wet—even your binoculars get wet. This binocular poncho puts an end to wet binoculars.

You'll need: a circular piece of heavy plastic large enough to cover the binoculars when hung around your neck
scissors
binoculars with neck strap

1. Cut two holes in the plastic to match up with the neck strap hooks on your binoculars.

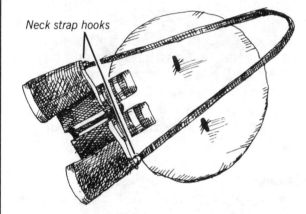

Neck strap hooks

2. Hook the neck straps into the binoculars through the holes.

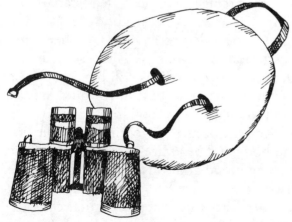

3. The poncho will hang down, covering the binoculars when they are not being used. When you want to use them, simply flip back the poncho.

Biters and stingers

When it comes to biting and stinging insects, it's a matter of "heads or tails." Some use their mouths to pierce your skin, while others use the opposite end. Whatever way they do it, it's usually the females who do the "dirty work." Here's why.

Mini-vampires

If you've been stabbed and jabbed by blood-sucking insects then you know how annoying, and sometimes painful, these mini-vampires can be. The needle-like mouth parts of insects like mosquitoes don't actually bite you—they pierce your skin. The female mosquito spits saliva into the wound to stop your blood from clotting and then she fills her "tank" with blood before flying off. Why are the females so bloodthirsty? Your blood is essential for the production of eggs in the female's body. So, like it or not, every bite may mean hundreds more mosquitoes to come.

Other flying blood-suckers to avoid include black flies, no-see-ums, deer flies and stable flies. Besides being irritating, some biters also carry diseases that they can pass on to people through their saliva.

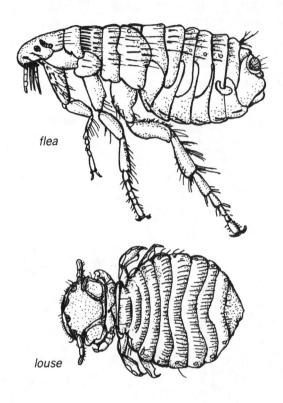

flea

louse

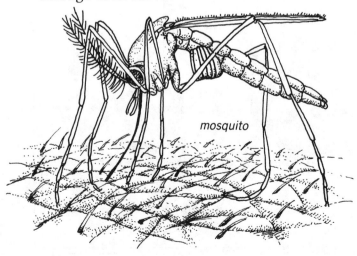

mosquito

Body bugs

Just thinking about fleas and lice can get you scratching. Fleas are wingless, hopping insects found in the hairs and feathers of many pets. And they're nearly impossible to catch—they jump 200 times their own body length in one bound. You're left scratching your head in frustration, and your pet is still scratching too! Occasionally, pets' fleas will bite people, but they won't hang around since you don't taste good to them.

Lice are not nice. Two kinds—pubic lice and body and head lice—can attack people, sucking blood and causing itching and discomfort. These lice, sometimes called "cooties," are tiny, flat insects that cling to your hair with their strong, curved claws.

Mind your own beeswax

When a bee stings, it's telling you to stay away, or mind your own beeswax. You are seen as a threat to the bee or the hive, and stinging is its best defence. Only female bees, wasps and some ants sting since the stinger is really the insect's ovipositor — the tube for laying eggs. Males don't have them. You may have heard that once a bee stings, it dies. This is true only for a honey bee. Its stinger has tiny barbs on it that get stuck in your skin. When the honey bee tries to pull the stinger out, its abdomen usually rips off and the bee dies. Other bees and wasps have smooth stingers that can go in and out like a needle, stinging many times. When you're stung, the insect injects poison from little glands in its abdomen. It's the poison that causes the irritation and swelling. Some people are highly allergic to bee stings and must see a doctor immediately.

Fighting back

Spraying and smearing insect repellents on your skin is one way of avoiding annoying bugs. Here are some others:

☐ *Wear long sleeves, long pants, hat and neck scarf.*

☐ *Buy or make a bug hat for really bad days (see page 124).*

☐ *Dress in light colours. Dark clothing seems to attract mosquitoes.*

☐ *Sit around a fire at night. Mosquitoes usually avoid smoke.*

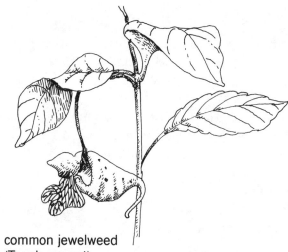

common jewelweed
(Touch-me-not)

Once bitten (or stung) . . .

If you've been bitten or stung, try one of these "home remedies" to relieve the pain or itching.

☐ *Jewelweed is a great anti-itching plant that grows in wet areas — right where the mosquitoes breed. Just break open a stem and rub the clear juice on your mosquito bite. The itching will stop almost instantly.*

☐ *A paste made from baking soda and water can be spread on stings or bites to relieve pain and control swelling.*

Insects in danger

How many people live in your town or city? If you live in a big city there may be more than a million people, or a small town may have only a few thousand. Now try to imagine the huge insect population. On average, there are about 200 000 insects for every one person on earth. Of course, just like small towns and big cities, the numbers are not evenly spread. In general, there are more insects in warm climates than in cold climates.

Even though there are lots of insects, some kinds are becoming endangered. Without help, these endangered insects may disappear from the earth forever. So what? Insects may not be everyone's favourite wildlife, but they are a vital part of the natural world and contribute a great deal to our way of life. They provide food for thousands of birds, mammals and fish, help pollinate flowers, fruits and vegetables and provide people with products such as honey and silk. Why are some insects becoming endangered?

Like many endangered species, some insects' biggest problem is the loss of habitat—a safe site for breeding, feeding and sheltering. Tropical rain forests, where more than half of all the world's insects live, are being destroyed. And wetland areas that are home to millions of insects are being drained. Insects are losing their homes!

For some insects their beauty is their worst enemy. Some of the most treasured collector's items are large and beautifully coloured butterflies and moths. Some collectors pay a lot of money for rare species. This only encourages people to look for them, kill and sell them. Unfortunately, the more endangered a species is, the more it is sought after.

Another problem for insects may be competition from new neighbours. Each country or part of a country has its own native species of plants and animals, including insects. Under natural conditions they all live together in a balanced ecosystem. But if you

introduce a new plant, animal or disease from a different country into an ecosystem, the balance may become upset. For example, starlings are the most abundant birds in North America today, but they've only been here since the late 19th century. An Englishman introduced the starling to North America because he wanted to have all the birds here that were in England. Unfortunately, many birds that were already here, such as the Eastern Bluebird, have suffered. Starlings outcompete bluebirds for nest holes and are partly to blame for a decline in the bluebird's population.

Save the insects!

Want to help, but don't know where to start? Here are some things you can do to save insects.

☐ Stop swatting and spraying every insect you see; learn how to live alongside them. Some insects, like mosquitoes, will always be pesty, but you needn't worry about ladybugs or praying mantids, so let them be.

☐ Concentrate on observing insects in nature, rather than collecting them.

☐ Support environmental groups that are working to protect endangered species by volunteering time or donating money to help pay for research and habitat protection. You can raise money by doing anything from washing cars to selling popcorn. And your money can make a difference. One nature club, Lambton Wildlife Incorporated, in Sarnia, Ontario, bought land where threatened karner blue butterflies live. Donations from individuals and conservation groups helped the club buy the land and save the species.

☐ Introduce some friends to the fascinating world of insects. Start a bug club at school and help teach the rest of the students about the importance of protecting insects. The more people know, the more they'll care and want to help.

☐ Find out what is being done in other countries to help protect insect habitats. For instance, tropical rain forests are home to thousands of kinds of insects. If the rain forests are destroyed, we will lose much of the diversity of insect life. International environmental groups such as World Wildlife Fund are working to save tropical rain forests in Central and South America. They use donations to help buy up rain forests and protect them forever.

Dyeing with plants

What colours are the clothes you're wearing right now? Chances are you've named several colours, all produced by commercial dyes. But if you had lived before these dyes became available in the 1850s, your clothes would probably have been coloured with natural dyes from plants. You can collect some common plants and try your hand at dyeing. The dandelions suggested here will produce a greenish-yellow colour but you may also want to try some of the other plants listed.

You'll need:
a sharp knife (Ask an adult to help you.)
1 kg (2 lbs) of dandelion leaves and
  stems
2 pots
water
5 mL (1 tsp) alum (available at a
  drugstore)
2 mL (1/2 tsp) washing soda (available at
  a grocery store)
a clean white t-shirt, clean scraps of
  cotton, or whatever material you want
  to dye
a pair of rubber gloves
a strainer

1. Chop the dandelion leaves and stems into small pieces. Place them in a pot, cover with water, and leave them to soak overnight.

2. In another pot, mix the alum and washing soda with 4 L (1 gallon) of water. Soak your cloth in this overnight. The alum and washing soda are called a mordant. This is a substance that helps bind the dye into the material to keep it from running when you wash your t-shirt. Wear rubber gloves when using the mordant because it will dry out your skin. It isn't necessary to use mordants when dyeing with lichens.

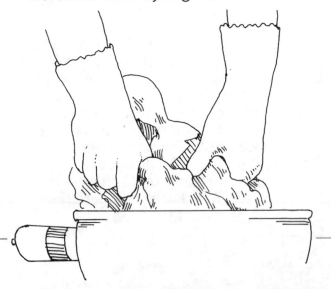

3. The next morning, simmer the plant and water mixture on medium heat for about an hour. If using roots or bark, simmer for 8 to 12 hours. Strain out the plant materials and put them aside. Let the dye water cool.

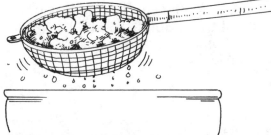

4. Wearing rubber gloves, remove your cloth from the mordant and gently squeeze it out.

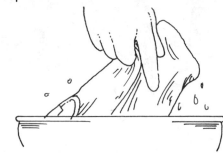

5. Place the cloth in the cooled dye water, add enough water to cover the material, and simmer for 10 to 20 minutes. If dyeing with roots or bark, simmer for 8 hours or more. The longer you simmer the cloth, the deeper the colour will be. The wet cloth will become a slightly lighter colour when dry.

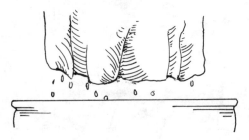

6. Rinse your cloth in hot water and then cool water, until the rinse water is clear. Hang your material to dry inside or in a shady place outside.

Some common plants for dyeing
Follow the same instructions for dyeing with the plants listed below.

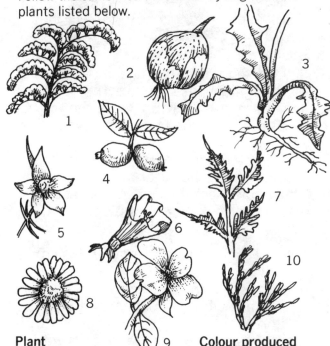

Plant	Colour produced
1. goldenrod flowers	yellow
2. onion skins	dark yellow
3. dandelion roots	red-violet
4. butternut husks	deep tan
5. larkspur petals	blue
6. red hollyhock flowers	pink
7. ragweed leaves	green
8. chamomile flowers	bright yellow
9. dogwood root bark	red
10. cedar root	purple

Sweet sap

If you like to dig into a pile of pancakes dripping with pure maple syrup, try making your own syrup. Once the weather has turned to warm days and cold nights in the early spring, you should be ready for action. Nature has already made the sugar-sweet sap inside the maple trees—all you have to do is get it out, cook it and eat it up.

You'll need:
a hand drill with an 11 mm (7/16 inch) drill bit
mature sugar maple trees
spiles (available at most hardware stores)
pails (large plastic ice-cream pails work well) with plastic bags for lids
string
a large pail or container
a large pot
a stove
Mason jars with lids
a sharp knife
small sticks
a hammer

1. Drill one or two holes in each maple tree at about waist height. If two holes are made in the same tree, drill them on opposite sides of the tree. An average tree will produce about 55 L (12 gallons) of sap over a three-week sap run. You'll need to collect a lot of sap—it takes about 180 L (40 gallons) of sap to make 5 L (1 gallon) of syrup.

2. Insert the spiles into the holes and hang the pails from the spiles. Tie a plastic bag over each pail and spile with string to help keep dirt and bugs out of your sap.

3. Collect the sap in your large container at least once a day.

4. Pour the sap into a large pot that you keep on simmer on your stove. As long as steam is rising from the pot, the water is evaporating from the sap and making it thicker. The pot must never boil dry, so keep adding sap as the level in the pot goes down.

5. As the sap thickens, it will turn from an almost colourless, watery liquid into an amber-coloured, concentrated syrup. Once you think it has reached the right taste and consistency, pour it into jars and seal them.

6. You can also make chewy maple taffy by pouring some hot syrup in a cup of clean snow. In a few seconds, you'll have a sweet, tasty candy to eat.

7. When the sap is finished running, or you've collected enough, remove the pails and spiles from the trees. Ask an adult to whittle a sharp point on one end of a small stick and hammer the stick into the hole left by the spile. This acts like a bandage for the tree.

Start a feather collection

You don't have to pluck a chicken to collect feathers. Birds moult at least once a year, and you can often find their feathers on the ground, especially near their nests. A feather collection can help you compare the feathers of different birds and different feathers of the same bird. You can also look at how the feather is constructed and coloured.

You'll need: feathers
several sheets of three-ring binder
   paper
glue or tape
a pen
clear plastic food wrap (optional)
a binder

1. Collect feathers and arrange them attractively on sheets of paper. You may wish to organize the feathers by size, colour or type of bird. Glue or tape the feathers to the paper.

2. Label each feather as well as you can. Include species (if known), where it was found (city and habitat) and when.

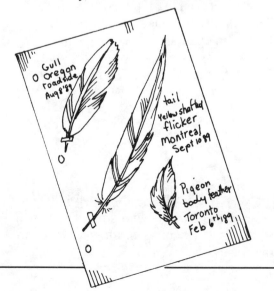

3. You can cover each page with a clear plastic wrapping to protect the feathers. Colours will fade over time.

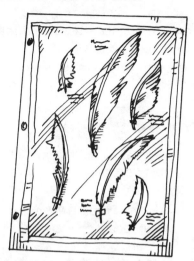

4. Store your collection in a binder.

Affordable bird housing

With a few simple materials you can become an architect for birds. By building one of these birdhouses you can attract a feathered family to your yard and watch the amazing transformation from egg to independent young.

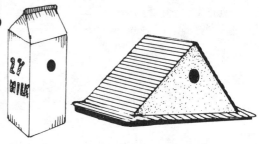

Milk carton birdhouse

Milk cartons are great for holding more than just milk. You can turn one into a "bird carton."

You'll need: a 2-L (or 2-quart) waxed cardboard milk carton
scissors
50 cm (20 inches) of strong but bendable wire
2 nails
a hammer
waterproof packing tape
dried grasses

1. Open up the top of the carton and wash it out well with warm water and a brush.
2. Cut out a circle 4 cm (1½ inches) in diameter on one side of the container, about 5 cm (2 inches) below the bend in the carton.

3. On the opposite side of the carton, poke two holes with a nail. The top hole should be one-third of the way down from the bend and the second hole about two-thirds of the way down.

4. Thread the wire into the top hole, down the carton on the inside, and out of the bottom hole.

5. Place a little bit of dried grasses in the bottom of the carton.
6. Seal the top of the carton back up with waterproof packing tape.
7. To put your birdhouse up, choose a pole or tree in an open area. Hammer your nails into the tree so that they are spaced about 30 cm (12 inches) apart, one above the other.

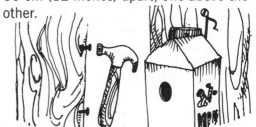

8. Wrap one end of the wire around each nail so that the birdhouse is firmly attached to the tree.

Popsicle stick birdhouse

After you've slurped away your Popsicle on a hot summer day, save the stick for a winter birdhouse building project. This easy-to-build house will attract nearby House Wrens.

You'll need: 72 Popsicle sticks
a 35 × 23 cm (14 × 9 inches) piece of cork, 10 mm (¼ inch) thick
a 26 × 10 cm (10¼ × 4 inches) piece of cork, 10 mm (¼ inch) thick
a sharp knife
white glue
a 26 × 10 cm (10¼ × 4 inches) piece of plywood, 10 mm (¼ inch) thick
3-4 nails
a hammer

1. Ask an adult to cut the cork, using a sharp knife. From the 35 × 23 cm (14 × 9 inches) piece, cut two triangles with all sides measuring 23 cm (9 inches).
2. In one cork triangle only, cut a hole 2.5 cm (1 inch) in diameter in the centre.

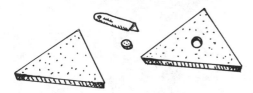

3. On your 26 × 10 cm (10¼ × 4 inches) piece of cork, glue 26 Popsicle sticks side by side, across the 26 cm (10¼ inch) side, so they are touching. This will form the floor of your birdhouse.

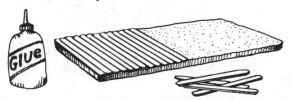

4. Glue your cork triangle with the hole, upright, on to the floor, about 12 mm (½ inch) from the front edge (long edge) and from each side.
5. Glue the solid cork triangle about 12 mm (½ inch) from the back edge.

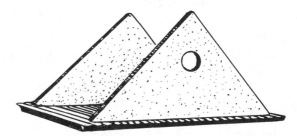

6. Glue 23 Popsicle sticks, side by side, on each side of the birdhouse so that they are attached to both front and back pieces of cork.
7. When you get to the peak, two sticks will meet. Put a bead of glue along the whole length of this join.

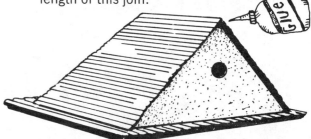

8. Set your plywood on a tree branch or pole near shrubs, about 2 m (6 feet) above the ground. Hammer the nails into the pole or tree to secure the wood.
9. Glue the bottom of your birdhouse to this wooden platform.

Birdfeeder checklist

You can keep track of the birds that live in your area or pass through during migration by making a bird checklist. It will help you remember which birds you saw and allow you to compare the number and kinds of birds from year to year. Scientists also keep these types of records to find out whether bird populations are going up or down and whether birds are moving into new areas.

A nearby birdfeeder is a good place to start your checklist. If the food is good, it's bound to attract lots of birds.

You'll need: a pad of paper
a pen or pencil
a field guide to birds
binoculars (if you have them)

1. Set up your paper in columns with these headings across the top: Species, No. of individuals, Date, Time, Weather, Remarks.

2. Choose the best spot in your house for watching your feeder and leave your chart and a pencil on a table nearby. Ask anyone who sees a bird at the feeder to fill in the chart.

3. At the end of the feeding season make a list of the different species of birds that visited your feeder. This list can be compared with those of past and future years. Use the other information to figure out the most popular time of day and best weather for feeding.

4. The same checklist can be used when you're birdwatching in the field. Carry a small pad of paper or use index cards for recording your findings.

Counting on birds

There are lots of birds out there to count.
About 645 species of birds live in North
America, north of Mexico. Some keen
birdwatchers, who keep a list of all the
different species they have ever seen (called a
Life List), have spotted 500 or more species.
Even an amateur can hope to see 300.

In some areas there are Birder Hotlines.
Phone into one of these hotlines and you'll hear
what new rare birds have been seen in the area.

Word travels like wildfire, and soon all the
local birdwatchers are on the lookout.

To get started on your bird counting
career, you might want to help out during a
local bird count. These are official days
established by naturalists' groups to count
birds in an area. And they can always use an
extra pair of eyes. Contact your local
naturalists' group for more information.

Gourmet bird food

You don't have to be a great chef to whip up something tasty for your feathered friends. Try this simple recipe and make a delicious seed salad for the birds. You'll find the seeds you need for it in a health food store or plant nursery.

Super seed salad

You'll need: 250 mL (1 cup) cracked corn
250 mL (1 cup) millet (white proso is popular)
250 mL (1 cup) sunflower seeds in shell (black-striped or oil)
100 mL (½ cup) buckwheat
100 mL (½ cup) shelled peanuts
50 mL (¼ cup) coarse white sand or fine gravel (see Stone salad below)

1. Mix the ingredients together.
2. Store in a dry place.

Wild salad

If you're planning a trip in the country in the fall, collect lamb's quarter, dock, smartweed and ragweed seeds in open fields and along roadsides. Shake the seeds into a paper bag and mix them into your Super Seed Salad when you get home. The birds will go wild over your wild salad.

Stone salad

Sand or fine gravel are important ingredients in your bird salad. Why? It helps birds grind up their food. Birds don't have teeth to crush and grind up their food so that they can digest it. Instead they swallow food whole and grind it up in a thick-walled, muscular part of the stomach called the gizzard. Small stones and sand in the gizzard help with the grinding. They are called "gizzard stones."

Feed a hummingbird

The dazzling acrobatic displays of hummingbirds are a treat to watch, so it's worth the effort to attract them to your garden. Fortunately, hummingbirds are suckers for nectar. They actually stick their long bills into flowers and suck up the sweet nectar inside. They prefer red, orange or purple flowers with tube- or bell-shaped blossoms. Morning glories, lilies, petunias, hollyhocks, trumpet creepers, bonfire and fuchsia are all hummingbird tempters. When planting flowers rich in nectar, you may get an added bonus: butterflies.

Hanging baskets of fuchsia, red impatiens or similar flowers are irresistible to hummingbirds. They will visit these "hanging gardens" even when people are nearby.

Natural birdfeeders
Instead of cleaning up the garden after the plants die, leave the flower stalks standing. They will serve as natural birdfeeders for the birds over the winter.

Follow the food

What happens to the seeds and nuts eaten by birds? You can track the food from beginning to end by following the numbers in this see-through Blue Jay.

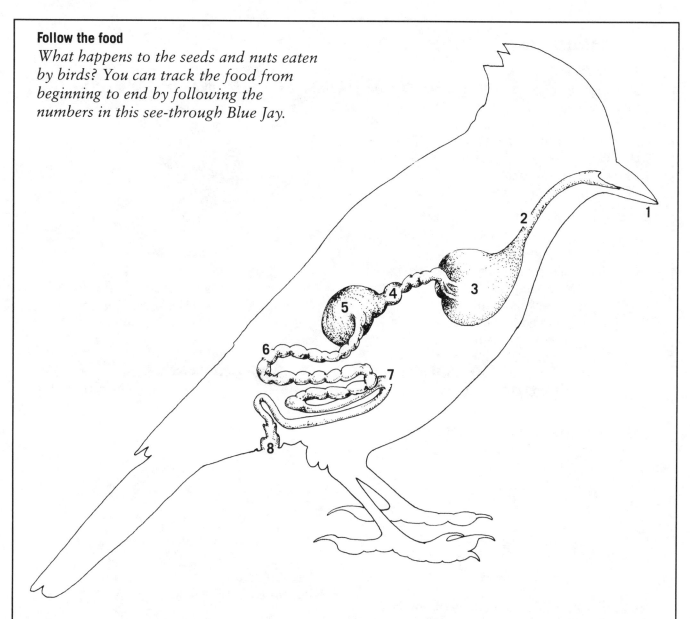

The seeds enter the bird's mouth (1) and travel down the esophagus (2) to the crop (3). The crop lets a bird pig out and store the food until later. Vultures, for instance, may eat so much at one sitting that their crop is overflowing. They may be too heavy to fly! The stored food can be digested when the bird is resting or sleeping, or it may be regurgitated and fed to baby birds.

From the crop, the food enters the stomach (4) and gizzard (5), where it is ground up. The food wastes that are not digested travel out of the bird by way of the small (6) and large intestines (7) and the cloaca (8). Some people call the result bird poop, but its technical name is guano.

A *humdinger of a hummingbird feeder*

How much do you drink in a day? Hummingbirds drink seven times their body weight each day. If you drank seven times *your* weight, you'd gulp down more than a hundred cans of pop a day! Because hummingbirds are so thirsty and so beautiful, many people make special feeders to attract them. This hummingbird feeder is easy to make and sure to be a hit.

You'll need: a clean baby-food jar with lid
a hammer
a large nail
red enamel paint
a small paintbrush
100-cm (40-inch) piece of thin, bendable wire
125 mL (½ cup) white sugar
600 mL (2½ cups) boiling water
red food colouring
a hook

1. Hammer the nail into the centre of the lid to make a hole about 3 mm (⅛ inch) across. Remove the nail.

2. Turn the lid over and hammer down the sharp edges around the hole.

3. Paint a pretty red flower around the hole on the top of the lid.

4. Fold the wire in two and wrap it around the neck of the jar twice. Twist the ends together to keep the wire around the jar neck.

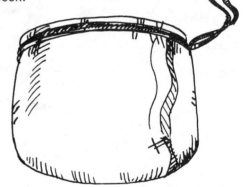

5. Stir the sugar into the water to make your nectar. Do not substitute honey for the sugar. Add a few drops of red food colouring. Let the mixture cool.

6. Pour the nectar into the jar and put the lid on. Put any leftover nectar in the fridge.

7. Twist the tail ends of the wire together and hang your feeder from a hook or nail on your verandah, eaves, or balcony or from a wooden support in your garden.

Your feeder needs to be washed out every week with a little vinegar and a scrub brush. Rinse with water and refill with fresh nectar. If a lot of insects feed on the nectar, rub a little vegetable oil around the opening of the feeder. It will help keep insects, but not hummingbirds, away.

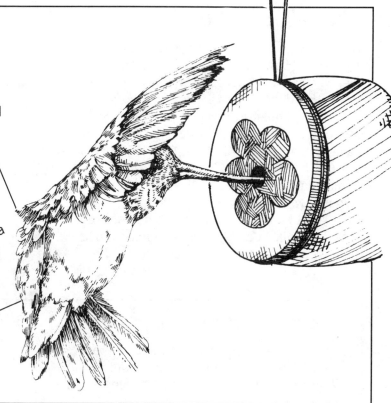

Hovering hummingbirds

How many times can you flap your arms in one second? Chances are you don't even come close to 75. That's how often a hummingbird flaps its wings in just one second. To make this possible, a hummingbird has huge chest muscles that give power to its wings. These flapping muscles make up one-third of the hummingbird's weight.

Hummingbirds are like tiny acrobats. They can fly up, down, backward, forward, sideways and even upside down. Because they hover in front of flowers or feeders, they are easy to watch—until they zip off to the next treat. As you watch a hummingbird fly by, you may hear the distinctive hum of its wings that gives it its name. The humming sound is caused by the vibration of the long primary feathers on the wings.

Hummingbirds eat mainly flower nectar and some insects, so hummingbirds from cold climates must migrate in winter when food becomes scarce. Even though they are among the smallest birds in the world, some hummingbirds fly a long way. The Rufous Hummingbird, for example, migrates between Alaska and Central America. That's a round trip of 8000 km (5000 miles) for a bird no bigger than your thumb!

Making a bird bath

With a few household materials you can make a great bird bath to keep your feathered friends clean and happy. Even in winter, birds still bathe and drink, so your bird bath can be a year-round meeting place. If the water in your bird bath freezes in winter, you'll need to rig up a heater. ASK AN ADULT TO HELP YOU BECAUSE THIS CAN BE DANGEROUS. Place a small aquarium heater in the bird bath and plug it in with a heavy-duty, outdoor extension cord. What happens when there is no unfrozen water to drink? Luckily, birds can quench their thirst by picking at snow and ice.

Bird bath tips

Your bird bath should have:
- a non-slippery surface (by thinly coating a surface with white glue and sprinkling sand over it, you will have a good surface)
- gently sloping sides
- a maximum depth of 8 cm (3 inches)
- some shade
- nearby dense vegetation for cover

Clean the bath often and keep it filled with water.

A hanging or sunken bird bath

This bird bath comes in two versions — a hanging bath and an in-ground model. Whichever you choose, your bird bath will be a hit with the locals.

You'll need: 2 pieces of binder twine, each about 1.2 m (4 feet) long
a large pottery plant saucer or large earthenware pie plate

1. Place your two pieces of twine on the floor to form an X. Make a knot where the twine meets.
2. Place your saucer on the twine so that the knot is beneath the centre of the saucer.

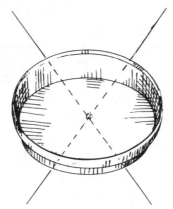

3. Carefully gather the four ends of the twine above the saucer and tie a double knot.
4. Hang your saucer from a branch and fill it with water.

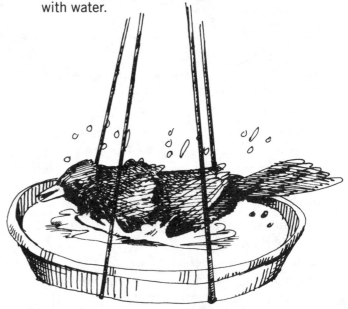

5. To make a sunken bird bath, place the saucer in a hole in the ground so that the edges are level with the ground.
WARNING: if there are neighbourhood cats around, use the hanging bird bath instead of the sunken version.

Wetcleaning, drycleaning and ants

Most birds, unlike some kids, love having a bath. In wild areas, birds look for ponds, streams and springs for bathing and drinking. Even birds passing overhead may make a pit stop if they hear the sound of running or dripping water. Most birds bathe to keep clean and to cool off during hot weather. Hummingbirds, however, take baths several times a day just for fun.

Many birds take two kinds of baths—a water bath to get clean and a dust bath to get rid of parasites, such as lice and mites. Some ornithologists (scientists who study birds)

believe that dust baths also help birds sandblast their feathers, cleaning them and restoring their insulation value.

Perhaps the strangest way some birds have of getting clean is by rubbing live ants into their feathers. Jays, robins, sparrows and other songbirds use their beaks to rub the ants in. Or they stand on an anthill and let the ants climb up onto their bodies. Sound like a scene from a science fiction movie? Some ornithologists think the ants produce certain chemicals that kill bird parasites.

An added attraction

Birds are enchanted by the sound of running or dripping water, so why not let them have it!

You'll need: a nail
a plastic bucket
a small piece of cotton material
60 cm (2 feet) of binder twine

1. Use the nail to poke a hole in the bottom of your bucket.
2. Stick the piece of cotton through the hole so that it hangs down.
3. Use the twine to hang your bucket in a tree directly over your bird bath.
4. Fill the bucket with water daily. The piece of cotton will soak up water and cause it to drip down into the bird bath.

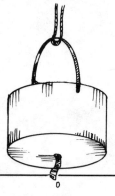

A dust bath

Sometimes birds like to give themselves a thorough "drycleaning" with dust. Here's how to make a dust bath.

You'll need: a shallow box
5-8 cm (2-3 inches) of roadside dust

1. Place the dust in the box.
2. Put the box in a sheltered area outside.
3. Refill the box as necessary.

Gardening for birds

Learning to be a good host or hostess to birds can be very rewarding and fun. If you give birds their four basic needs for survival, they will be only too happy to spend time in your yard. You must provide **food**, **water**, **shelter** where birds can hide from predators and bad weather and a safe and suitable **nesting area**. Backyard habitats can range from several hectares or acres right down to a verandah or window box. Here are some tips to get you started.

Size it up

As you're choosing plants to put into your garden, keep in mind that different birds prefer different sizes of flowers, bushes and trees.
- Red-eyed Vireos, tanagers and orioles prefer tall trees.
- Thrashers and cardinals nest in shrubs of medium height.
- Song Sparrows and Rufous-sided Towhees like low-growing plants.

In addition to varying heights, you will attract more species if you provide both dense cover and open area.

Gourmet gardening

Food is a main attraction for birds. By serving a smorgasbord of different foods, birds can pick and choose the food that they require.
- Robins and Cedar Waxwings will be delighted with a feast of berries.
- Cone feeders such as crossbills are attracted to conifers like pine and hemlock or alders and birch trees.
- Blue Jays, woodpeckers and even squirrels can be lured with the promise of a good acorn harvest from an oak tree.

Planting trees and shrubs is an excellent way to provide a variety of food and habitat for birds, but it takes good planning and lots of work and it can be expensive. Most of all it takes time. Many trees must grow for at least five years to provide suitable shelter and food. Shrubs are usually much faster growing and may be occupied within a year.

Flower power

For a faster, easier and cheaper source of food and cover, try flowers. They offer a rainbow of colour to beautify your garden and also provide seeds or nectar to satisfy hungry birds. Choose flowers that are suited to your local climate. Also choose flowers that will flourish in your garden's mini-climate: some flowers like shady areas, others prefer sunshine. The necessary information is usually on the back of seed packages.

Planting annuals (plants that die at the end of the growing season) is a good way to attract birds. Annuals produce large quantities of seeds, which serve as food for such birds as American Goldfinches and Dark-eyed Juncos. Popular annuals include sunflowers, zinnias, cosmos and asters.

Where to plant

When you hear someone say, "Tallest at the back and smallest at the front," you probably think of a group photo. But flowers can be planted the same way. Very tall varieties of sunflowers and zinnias, for example, look best at the back of a flower bed and provide a background for lower blooms. Some tall plants may need support. They can be propped up against fences or tied to stakes. Climbing plants, such as morning glories, will need support too. They do well near a wall they can climb. Whatever and wherever you're planting, think clumps. Plant a large clump of similar flowers together. This gives birds a large food supply in a small area. And always plant near shelter. Birds won't visit wide-open spaces far from a safe shelter.

Mini-gardens

Even if you have very limited space, or no yard at all, you can create a mini-garden with flower pots or a window box. Plant some attractive flowers with foliage in a window box, add a small dish of water and a container of birdseed and—presto!—you have a tiny habitat for birds. Or group together an assortment of flower pots containing different sizes and colours of annuals on front steps or wherever there is room.

Bothersome birds

Have you got competition for the cherries, strawberries or peaches in your garden? It's not surprising that some birds also like to harvest your crops; summer fruits taste good to them, too. How can you discourage birds from freeloading in your fruit and vegetable gardens without driving them away from the rest of your yard? A few harmless, homemade creations should do the trick.

Scarecrow

This "bird discourager" is fun to make and adds character to your garden. Traditionally scarecrows have been stuffed with straw, but you can also use cotton rags or even scrunched-up plastic bags.

You'll need: an old broom
a coat hanger (wood or plastic)
heavy tape
an old, plain pillow case
string and scissors
felt markers
old clothes (long-sleeved shirt, jeans, hat and gloves)
lots of straw, old rags or plastic bags for stuffing
elastic bands

1. Attach a coat hanger to the broom as shown. Fasten it on securely with heavy tape.

2. Put a pillow case over the straw part of the broom. Stuff this head with straw, old rags or bunched-up plastic bags. Tie it shut with string.

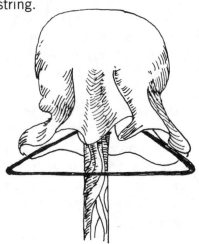

3. Draw on a face with felt markers and put on a hat.

4. Dress your scarecrow in old clothes. Use safety pins to attach the pants to the shirt. Stuff the clothes and tie the openings closed.

5. Choose a good spot in the garden for your scarecrow. "Plant" the broom handle into the ground.

6. For added effect, tie foil plates or tinsel to the hat or arms to help discourage birds. A fake owl sitting on the scarecrow's shoulder might also keep the birds from raiding your garden.

Tinfoil trees

Many birds are frightened by shining objects that move around or make noise. You can help to protect your fruit trees by hanging several foil pie plates from the branches, using string. The easier they swing in the breeze, the better. You might also try putting wind chimes in the tree to discourage the birds.

Operation rescue

If you find a young bird alone in the grass, what do you do? In most cases, the answer should be, "Nothing." Although the bird may look abandoned, its parents may be watching it from a nearby bush, gathering food or looking after other young. Hawk, owl, woodpecker and songbird chicks leave the nest before they can fly or take care of themselves. They are called altricial birds. The parents still look after them, but are not always visible. Other birds, such as ducks, geese, plovers and grouse, can look for food when they are only a few hours old. They are called precocial birds. Although out alone, they are still largely defenceless and their parents continue to care for them. So, if you find a bird and suspect it is an orphan, watch it carefully for an hour or so to be sure the parents aren't nearby. Only then should you think about caring for it yourself.

Giving a lift
Strong winds may blow a nestling or nest out of a tree. The nest should be put back in the tree as high as you can reach. A nestling should be returned to its nest, if possible. If the baby bird seems cold, cup your hands around it to warm it up. Once the bird is back in bed, place a hand over the nest to make it appear dark. This will help calm the bird and encourage it to snuggle down into the nest. Parents will not abandon their young just because you have touched them. Adult birds may, however, abandon a nest if it is disturbed during construction or soon after the eggs are laid.

A helping hand
If you do find an orphaned bird, take it indoors and give it shelter, warmth and food. A young altricial bird is like a human baby; it needs almost constant attention and eats a great deal. The best thing for the bird is for you to contact an animal care expert as soon as possible. In the meantime, here are some tips for keeping your guest happy and healthy.

A new nest
Make a cosy nest for the bird in a berry box or similar small container. Use shredded paper towels or tissues for a soft lining. Mother birds keep their babies warm by cuddling them close to their bodies. You will have to be the mother in this case and provide heat for the young bird. Put the new nest on a heating pad set on low or hang a light bulb over the nest. Very young birds with few or no feathers need a temperature of about 35° C (95° F). Down-covered nestlings should be kept at about 27° C (80° F).

Fast food

Very young birds should be fed every 15 minutes during daylight hours; otherwise, they'll slowly starve. But birds with feathers may only need to eat once an hour. Do not give water to young birds. What do you feed a baby bird? Try the recipes in the box on this page.

If you are caring for an adult bird, try to identify it. Use a good bird book to find out what it normally eats. Pet stores sell meal worms for insect eaters and seed mixtures for seed eaters. If you are not sure what to provide, give a bit of everything and let the bird decide. Leave the food out so the adult bird can feed on its own and provide a shallow dish of water for drinking and bathing.

Baby bird formula

This recipe is for helpless (altricial) baby birds, such as owls, hawks and songbirds.

You'll need: 25 mL (2 tbsp) water
25 mL (2 tbsp) milk
2 egg yolks
Pablum
vitamin drops

1. Mix the water, milk and egg yolks together in the top of a double boiler. Put water in the bottom of the double boiler and cook for 10 minutes over medium heat.
2. Add Pablum, a little at a time, until mixture is thick.
3. Add two or three vitamin drops and stir.
4. Use a large-holed medicine dropper for feeding.

Baby food for ducks and geese

Since the babies of some birds, such as ducks, geese, plovers and grouse, can eat by themselves, your job is easier.

You'll need: 3 hard-boiled egg yolks

1. Finely chop the yolks and spread them on a rough surface, such as wood.
2. Let the young bird scratch and feed as long as it wants.

Letting go

Try to get an animal care expert to look after any wildlife you find in trouble. If you must adopt it temporarily, don't forget that your orphan is a wild creature, not a pet. Young birds should be released back into their natural habitat as soon as their tail feathers grow in. Adults can be freed when they are able to look after themselves. In many areas there are laws against keeping wild birds. You may even need a permit to nurse an injured bird back to health. Call a local wildlife officer or conservation officer for information.

151

Bird-proofing your windows

Have you ever accidentally walked into sliding glass doors without seeing them? Large, clean windows are beautiful to look through but they can be dangerous, especially for birds. Why would a bird hit your window?

- The reflection of flowers and shrubs in the window confuses the bird. Believing another garden lies ahead, the bird flies into the window.
- A male bird may see its own reflection and think there is a competing male invading its territory. It then flies at the window to attack the intruder.
- Sometimes windows are arranged in a house so that there appears to be a passage right through the house. A bird in the backyard may think it can fly right through to the front yard . . . until it hits the window.

Hang-ups

Help prevent the injury and death of birds, especially during migration, by trying one or all of these ideas.

1. Hang tinkling or glittering objects in problem windows. Try strips of tin foil or wind chimes.
2. Reduce reflection by tacking up some light, see-through screening over the glass.
3. Make a hawk to put up in your window. Visiting songbirds will think it is a real predator and be very careful to avoid the window.

You'll need: a sheet of thin white paper for tracing
glue
light cardboard, from a cereal box or gift box
scissors
black magic-marker or crayon
30 cm (1 foot) of string
tape
thumb tack

1. Trace this hawk onto a piece of paper.
2. Glue the paper onto some light cardboard.
3. Cut the cardboard to the shape of the hawk.
4. Colour your hawk dark black on both sides.
5. Tape a string to the hawk's head and attach the other end of the string to the outside of your window frame using a thumb tack. Your hawk will work best if it can move freely in the wind.

First aid

If you find a bird that has become stunned or hurt after hitting a window, take it indoors and place it in a medium-sized covered box. After a few hours' rest it will probably be recovered and you can let it go. For more serious injuries see **Operation rescue** on pages 150–151.

Make a gull-go-round

Follow these simple instructions and create a gull-go-round to hang in your room.

You'll need: tracing paper
a pencil
glue
white bristol board
scissors
felt markers
a field guide to birds
string: 4 pieces 15 cm (6 inches)
   long and 4 pieces 25 cm (10
   inches) long
a dinner plate
a thumb tack

1. Trace the outline of this gull onto tracing paper.
2. Glue the traced gull onto a piece of bristol board and cut out the gull shape. You now have a pattern with which to draw your gulls.
3. Place the gull pattern on the bristol board and trace the outline. Do this eight times to make eight gulls.

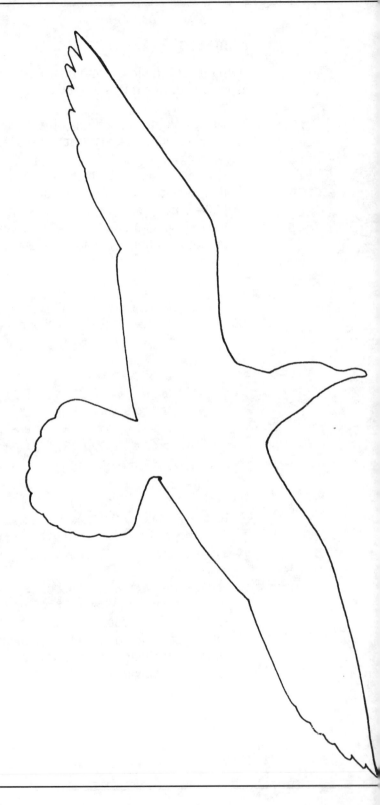

4. Cut out your gulls and colour each one as a different species, using a field guide for reference.

5. Use the sharp end of your scissors to punch a small hole in the top wing of each gull. Thread one piece of string through each hole, securing it with a knot. You will end up with four gulls on long strings and four gulls on short strings.

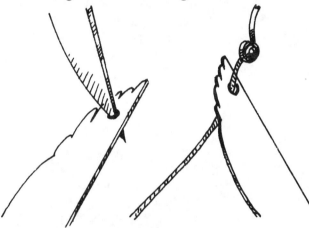

6. To make the disk from which to hang the gulls, trace the outline of a dinner plate on a piece of bristol board. Cut out the dinner-plate-sized circle.

7. Using the pointed end of your scissors, make eight evenly spaced holes along the outer edge of the disk. Make a final hole in the middle.

8. Tie the string from each gull through one of the outer holes, alternating long and short strings.

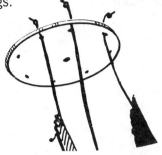

9. Use a thumb tack to suspend your gull-go-round from the ceiling.

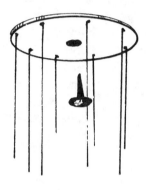

The red spot

Draw a red spot on the bottom half of some of your gulls' beaks. Some species, such as the Herring Gull, have this red spot. When a chick is hungry, it pecks at the spot, which signals the adult to regurgitate food for its young. Imagine if you could just press a button on the refrigerator and get fed!

Index

Answers

Tree totalling, page 30
The tree is 41 years old.

Branching out, page 31
The pine tree is 8 years old.

Busy bees (and wasps), page 54–55
Wax works: honey bee
Paper nests: paper wasp
Wrapping paper: hornet
Organ pipes: mud-dauber wasp
Pottery nests: potter wasp

Who's an insect and who isn't?, page 68
The real insects are: grasshopper, beetle, water strider, butterfly, mosquito, bristletail

Take a peek at a beak, page 88
The pelican eats fish; the hummingbird eats nectar; the swift eats insects; the cardinal eats seeds; the waxwing eats berries; the hawk eats mice (and other small animals).

Federation of Ontario Naturalists

Since 1931, the Federation of Ontario Naturalists (FON) has been protecting parks, forests, wetlands and wildlife. It has also been teaching people of all ages about the wonders of nature and how they can get involved in conservation activities. In recognition of the FON's work on behalf of nature and naturalists, Environment Canada recently presented the Federation with a National Environmental Achievement Award. The FON is supported by more than 15 000 members and local nature clubs. It also works with other provincial nature organizations as a member of the Canadian Nature Federation.

Join In!

Families across the country can join the Federation of Ontario Naturalists and enjoy its quarterly nature and environment magazine, *Seasons,* along with a special supplement specifically for children. Members can also have fun on one of the many informative and exciting nature excursions that operate across Ontario, as well as nationally and internationally. Summer nature camps for adults and children are another way to get involved in learning about nature and how to protect it.

For information on how to become a member of the FON or to receive a free catalogue of nature books, posters, education kits and gift items, just fill out the coupon on the following page and mail it in.

To get involved with the FON just fill
out this coupon and send it to:

Federation of Ontario Naturalists
355 Lesmill Road
Don Mills, ON
M3B 2W8

(Clip or photocopy this form)

Yes, I want to support the Federation of Ontario Naturalists.

Please send me membership information right away.

Name: _____

Address:_____

City: _____

Province: _____   Postal code: _____   Phone number: _____

❏ Please send me a copy of your free catalogue.

ase send me information on your trips and summer camps.